FORTRESS 113

THE MOSCOW KREMLIN

RUSSIA'S FORTIFIED HEART

MARK GALEOTTI

ILLUSTRATED BY DONATO SPEDALIERE

Series Editor Marcus Cowper

OSPREY

Bloomsbury Publishing Plc

Kemp House, Chawley Park, Cumnor Hill, Oxford OX2 9PH, UK

29 Earlsfort Terrace, Dublin 2, Ireland

1385 Broadway, 5th Floor, New York, NY 10018, USA

E mail: info@ospreypublishing.com

www.ospreypublishing.com

OSPREY is a trademark of Osprey Publishing Ltd

First published in Great Britain in 2022

© Osprey Publishing Ltd, 2022

A catalogue record for this book is available from the British Library.

ISBN: PB 9781472845498; eBook 9781472845504;

ePDF 9781472845474; XML 9781472845481

22 23 24 25 26   10 9 8 7 6 5 4 3 2 1

Index by Zoe Ross

Maps by www.bounford.com

Artwork illustrations by Donato Spedaliere

Originated by PDQ Media, Bungay, UK

Printed and bound in India by Replika Press Private Ltd

A NOTE ON LANGUAGE

Translating out of Cyrillic always poses challenges. I have chosen to transliterate other than well-known names as they are pronounced (so the letter ё becomes yo) and have ignored the diacritical 'soft' and 'hard' signs in the original. I also pluralize most words with an -s rather than a -i/-y, Russian-style, again other than those where the Russian plural has become standard. Although today the capital of Ukraine is known as Kyiv, I use the Russian form Kiev for all references relating to the period before 1991.

GLOSSARY AND ABBREVIATIONS

Bashnya – Tower, superseding earlier words such as *strelnitsa* and *vezha* from the 16th century

Bolverk – Redoubt

Boyevoi khod – 'Fighting walk', wall-top galleries

Detinets – Citadel, an archaic word superseded by *kremlin* by around the 14th and 15th centuries

Dvor – An estate, and later a courtyard

FSB – *Federal'naya sluzhba bezopasnosti*, Federal Security Service

FSO – *Federal'naya sluzhba okhrany*, Federal Protection Service

Gorod – Fortified settlement, later simply a town

KGB – *Komitet gosudarstvennoi bezopasnosti*, Committee of State Security

Kreml' – Kremlin, a fortress or citadel within a city; when not used in another context, it means the Moscow Kremlin

Krepost – Fortress or bastion

Otvodnaya strelnitsa – 'Diversionary tower', a bastion built to guard the far side of a bridge

Ploshchad' – Square

Podol – The 'hem' of a city, a shanty town or other unplanned, low-status housing outside the walls

Posad – A mercantile neighbourhood of a city, often outside the walls, occupied by artisans and traders

Slukh – 'Hearing', an underground chamber from which to listen for enemy tunnelling

Strelets – 'Shooter', arquebus-armed member of first Russian standing army (pl: *Streltsy*)

CONTENTS

INTRODUCTION   4

CHRONOLOGY   5

THE MOSCOW GOROD   6
The first settlements
Princely Moscow
The rise of Moscow

A WHITE-STONE FORTRESS   15
The age of the gun

RED-BRICK KREMLIN   18
Ivan the Terrible's Kremlin
Matryoshka Moscow
1571: fire

TIMES OF TROUBLES   30
A Polish fortress (briefly)
1682: rising
Capital no more

NAPOLEON AND NICHOLASES   36
Burning Moscow
Rebuilt, repurposed

RED FORTRESS   39
1905: the holdout
1917: Bolshevik target
Soviet power
Great Patriotic War
The Kremlin in the nuclear age

TWENTY TOWERS   48

TODAY'S KREMLIN   59
The Presidential Regiment

BIBLIOGRAPHY   63

INDEX   64

THE MOSCOW KREMLIN

INTRODUCTION

A fortified complex covering 28 hectares (70 acres) at the heart of Moscow, behind walls up to 19m high and watched over by 20 towers, the Kremlin houses everything from Russia's seat of political power to glittering churches. Built on the defensible Borovitsky Hill where the River Moskva meets the now-underground Neglinnaya River, it is an irregular triangle now flanked by the Moskva, Red Square and the Alexandrovsky Gardens.

This is a fortress that has evolved over time, from a pagan-era stockade to an 11th-century wooden guard tower and the current stone and brick complex, over the years having been built, burned, besieged and rebuilt. It has even changed colour, the original white limestone walls becoming today's rich red. It is also the largest still-active fortress in Europe.

It became a symbol first of the rising principality of Muscovy, then of the Romanov imperial state until 1713, when it ceded power to its new-built rival St Petersburg for just over two centuries. The revolutionary Soviet regime again made it the centre of the state, a role it still plays in Vladimir Putin's new Russia. Although often confused with the many-cupolaed St Basil's Cathedral (officially, the Cathedral of Vasily the Blessed)

This image, taken as Mil Mi-8AMTSh helicopters fly over Moscow during the 2020 Victory Day air show, clearly shows the layout of the complex, with the Beklemishevskaya Tower in the bottom left. Note the helicopter pads in the Secret Garden. (Sergei Bobylev\TASS via Getty Images)

standing at one end of Red Square, the Kremlin's neo-Gothic towers and swallowtail walls remain an enduring landmark.

It has been the eye of hurricanes of war and raid, razed by Mongols, mined by Napoleon, and battered by Nazi bombers. Even today, the elite Presidential Regiment is housed behind its walls in the green-roofed and yellow-fronted Arsenal building, and the defences of the seat of Russian government have moved into the invisible realms of the ether, with drone and GPS jamming systems and complex cyber defences. Protected by the aircraft and missiles of the Moscow Air Defence Region – no civil aircraft are allowed to fly over the centre of the city – and connected by tunnels to distant command centres and Vnukovo airport, the Kremlin is still at the heart of the Russian security state.

The Kremlin from across the Moskva, showing the walls and the Annunciation Tower in the foreground, with the massive Grand Kremlin Palace behind, and the Ivan the Great Belltower to the right. (Author's collection)

CHRONOLOGY

1147	Official date of foundation, by Yuri Dolgoruky
1156	Construction of new wooden *gorod* begins
1238	Moscow conquered by Mongols
1272	Moscow assigned to Prince Daniil Aleksandrovich
1293	Moscow *gorod* burned by Mongols
1325	Metropolitan moves to Kremlin
1339	Kremlin rebuilt in wood
1366–68	Kremlin rebuilt in limestone
1368, 1379	Lithuanian sieges
1382	Golden Horde sacks Kremlin
1485–95	Kremlin rebuilt in brick
1535–38	Kitay-Gorod walls built
1571	Great Fire of Moscow
1586–93	Bely Gorod walls built
1591	Skorodom walls built
1610–12	Polish occupation
1638–41	Zemlyannoy Val walls built
1713	Capital moves from Moscow to St Petersburg
1812	Napoleon's occupation
1905	Failed revolution in Moscow
1917	Successful revolution in Moscow
1918	Bolsheviks move capital back to Moscow Kremlin
1941–42	Kremlin bombed in World War II
1962	Metro-2 operational
1991	Dissolution of USSR: Kremlin becomes seat of new Russian Federation government

THE MOSCOW GOROD

The first settlements

The Borovitsky Hill on the high left bank of the River Moskva, tucked into its confluence with the Neglinnaya River (now underground), is to this day a commanding location, reaching 145m above sea level, at once defensible and connected. After all, the waterways were once the main communications routes through the thick Russian forest, and the Moskva flows into the Oka, and thence the mighty Volga, leading all the way south to the Caspian Sea.

It has thus long been a site of trade and settlement. Archaeological finds date its first occupation back at least as far as the Neolithic era, with stone axes and bone fishing hooks of the Lyalovo culture, from the 4th millennium BC. They did not necessarily settle here, though, but the later Fatyanovo nomadic herder culture from the 3rd millennium BC onwards built winter villages on hills such as Borovitsky, saddle-roofed log houses connected by wooden tunnels. The Bronze Age Fatyanovo peoples were in due course supplanted by the Dyakovo culture of around the 7th century BC to the 7th century AD. These Iron Age Finno-Ugric tribes of the Merya peoples were farmers and cattle-herders, their villages surrounded by wooden palisades.

The imposing Borovitskaya Tower sits on the part of Moscow that has probably been inhabited the longest, the crown of the Borovitsky Hill. (A. Savin/CC 3.0)

One appears to have been built in what is now Cathedral Square in the heart of the Kremlin complex. It was ultimately superseded – by conquest or simple displacement – by a larger settlement of the Vyatiches, East Slavs hailing from the Oka basin, who by around the 8th century AD had begun a slow colonization of the region. By the beginning of the 10th century, they had established their own village atop the Borovitsky Hill. The old village was expanded into a larger one surrounded by a moat and stockade, and a smaller one to the south-west, on the most elevated point, overlooking the confluence of the Moskva and Neglinnaya Rivers. This was likely the higher-status fastness of a local chieftain or perhaps a religious figure. Either way, this was also protected by its own moat and stockade. Beyond it, the Vyatiches practised slash-and-burn agriculture, clearing swathes of forest by fire and blade for cultivation, then new fields when the soil's fertility declined.

While no more than a large village, the settlement prospered, thanks to the trade along the Moskva, and also a ford at the foot of the hill, where

---

A 12TH-CENTURY GOROD

Ivan Dolgoruky's 12th-century Kremlin was as much township as fortress, with the oak-beamed walls of the *gorod* enclosing both his own citadel as well as churches, orchards and the estates of the prince's followers and more substantial Muscovites. Atop a cleared space in the deep Russian forest, the town is only just beginning its ascent to power as a trading as well as political hub, although a mark of its rise is the fire to the north-east, as a clearing is burned out of the forest to allow more farming in the new year. Although the Moskva and Neglinnaya Rivers are frozen in the deep winter, sleighs can still use them to move goods and pass on information.

today stands the Bolshoi (Large) Kamenny Bridge. Two land routes developed, one to the thriving mercantile centre of Novgorod to the north-west, the other to Kiev, the dominant Russian city of the time, far to the south-west. Archaeological finds in the smaller citadel, for example, included an 11th-century Kievan seal. Around the two main settlements there formed a *podol*, an unplanned sprawl of huts and homesteads for merchants, and those who fed and served them: potters and blacksmiths, swine-herds and butchers, bakers and basket-weavers. Beyond the *podol*, off the hill, the 10th- and 11th-century burial mounds found in the area, *kurgans*, attest to the pre-Christian faith of the Vyatiches and the neighbouring Kriviches, one dominated by deities of sun, storm and earth.

In AD 988, Prince Vladimir of Kiev had his troops march his people at spear-point into the Dnieper River to be forcibly baptized. Christianity was imposed as the new faith, and pagan idols were tumbled into the same river. Over the next decades and centuries, Christianity would spread across the Russian lands, especially encouraged by princes, for whom this was both a mark of modernity and also a form of social control, relying on the priests to help them control their once-pagan people. This was also visible in the geographies of power, as fortifications, palaces and churches grew together.

'Kremlin'

Russian has many words for fortresses and walled settlements, which changed in use over time. A *kreml'* is really a fortress inside a city (often walled in its own right), and the term only came into widespread use in the 14th century. Before then, terms such as *detinets* (citadel) and simply *gorod* (town) were as often common. The roots of the word are disputed. To some, it comes from the Greek *kremnos*, meaning a cliff, as such a fortress was usually built on a city's highest point. To others, though, its origins are from the Russian *kremen'*, meaning flint, denoting hardness.

Princely Moscow

The first mention of Moscow in the chronicles, which are still our best guide to the early medieval era, is from 1147, which has been adopted as the official year of foundation. Then, it was a small princely estate, quite possibly a hunting lodge, owned by the principality of Vladimir-Suzdal. According to an account that survives only in secondary sources, it was the estate of one Kuchko, a boyar (aristocrat) of Suzdal who quarrelled with Yuri Dolgoruky (Yuri the Long-Armed), son of the Grand Prince of Kiev and prince of Vladimir-Suzdal. The original claim was that the cause of the feud was that Dolgoruky had slept with Kuchko's wife; a later version was that he had refused to bow his head when the prince passed. Either way, the upshot was that Kuchko lost his wife, head and estate.

In 1147, Dolgoruky conducted a successful military campaign against the rival cities of Novgorod and Smolensk, in alliance with Prince Svyatoslav Olgovich of Belgorod-Seversky. According to the Primary Chronicle, Dolgoruky then extended an invitation to Svyatoslav: 'Come, my brother, to Moscow.' Svyatoslav accepted and the Chronicle

President Putin had a statue of his namesake Prince Vladimir, who brought Christianity to Russia, erected close to the Kremlin – the Trinity Tower is visible in the background. (Author's collection)

details his arrival, accompanied by his two sons and an escort drawn from his *druzhina*, a prince's armed retinue. Feasting and an exchange of gifts followed, but the fact that two princes and their immediate followers could comfortably be entertained suggests this was an estate of some substance.

Legends of the rise

Predictably enough, a variety of myths arose as to how, why and when Moscow was founded. *The Tale of Oleg, Founder of Moscow*, also known as *Of the Beginnings of the Sovereign Town of Moscow* (which actually seems to be a late 17th century creation), claims the city was established in AD 880 by a henchman of Rurik, the Varangian – Viking – warlord and adventurer who invaded Russia in the 9th century AD. Oleg was regent to Rurik's son Igor and later became replaced by him, going on to seize Kiev from two other Varangians, Askold and Dir. There is, however, no evidence to support the claim he also founded Moscow. Even more fanciful is the *Tale of the Rise of Moscow and of the Krutitsy Eparchy*, which sets the founding in 1212, and appeared around the same time as *The Tale of Oleg*. Here, a mythical Prince Daniil is looking for the right place to found a city when he encounters a three-headed beast with a spotted pelt. His trusted advisor, Basileios the Greek, interprets this as an omen: the three heads demonstrate that his future citadel will be triangular, and the spots represent the heterogeneity of its population.

Whether because of greater trade or princely patronage, the population of Moscow began to grow. In around 1156, a new *gorod*, or fortified settlement – the word later simply came to mean town in Russian – began to be built atop the hill. This is generally ascribed to Dolgoruky himself, although the evidence suggests he was actually still in Kiev at the time. It is more likely that he simply gave the orders and his son Andrei Bogolyubsky (Andrei the Pious) actually supervised the work.

An earthern rampart 7m high and 14–15m wide, surrounded a site of around 3 hectares (just under 8 acres). An oak wall surmounted the berm, made *gorodnya*-style, of interlocking trunks forming hollow shells which were then filled with soil. They were 'two spear lengths' high' and broad enough that covered *boyevoi khod* ('fighting walk') galleries (also called *polats*) were built all round them on duckboards. A 5m-deep moat was dug

No wooden fortifications from the early days of Moscow survive, but the Moss Tower from the fortress-prison of Sumy on the shores of the White Sea, while built in the 1500s, is similar to those of earlier centuries, made of wooden logs carefully interlocked. (Author's collection)

In its own way, this fragment of an icon illustrating a battle between Novgorod and Suzdal in 1170 illustrates the realities of conflicts at the time, with relatively small armies based around mounted princely *druzhina*s supported by poorly armed and often equally poorly motivated infantry levies. (Public domain)

beyond the wall. Inside that wall, Bogolyubsky built himself a citadel, also of oak beams. This was a pyramid-roofed tower within a stockade of its own, a fence of sharpened logs enclosing a market garden, outbuildings and stables for his *druzhina*. It was perhaps the first true *kremlin* – fortress – on the site, and marked the slow rise of Moscow.[1] Like most such *gorod*s, the walls enclosed not only the princely estate but also the homes of priests, artisans and merchants. Typically each was its own *dvor* (homestead, later meaning courtyard): a house and smallholding, surrounded by a *tyn*, a lath or log fence.

At this stage, there was no real garrison, as such. A prince had his *druzhina*, but one resident in such a small town as Moscow would have only a few dozen such professional warriors, and they would mainly travel with their lord. These were rough and dangerous times, though, and most adult men could also find and wield an axe, spear or bow if needed. Such militias were the mainstay of the defence of all but the largest and richest towns, and from time to time were also pressed or paid to serve in expeditions to raid other towns.

This was, however, still a small, remote settlement: a cleared hill amidst a trackless forest of bramble-choked pine, oak and birch. In 1176, for example, rival warbands from Chernigov and Vladimir supposedly managed to march past each other as well as the town in the winter fog. Nonetheless, there were signs of future glory. In 1264, it became a princely seat in its own right. Early Russian princes often moved from city to city, between conquests

[1] See FOR 61: *Medieval Russian Fortresses, AD 862–1480*

B MONGOLS RAZING THE KREMLIN IN 1293

As part of a punitive sweep through Central Russia, the Golden Horde general, Tudan, led an army to sack a chain of cities. In 1293, they took on Moscow, after five days of siege. Having breached the walls, Mongol soldiers storm through Moscow, killing and burning as they go. Facing fire and death, the city's defenders resist as best they can, but are outnumbered and outmatched. The population is largely butchered, and the town and its church virtually burned to the ground.

Since the days of Ivan III, the village of Kolomenskoye, south-east of the Kremlin, has been a royal estate. The reconstructed palace includes later features such as glass windows, but gives a sense of classic Russian wooden architecture, and in particular the Grand Ducal Palace inside the Kremlin. (Author's collection)

and patrimonies held by their bloodline, 'trading up' when they could, forced to 'downsize' when they lost some military or political confrontation. Alexander Nevsky, for example, was especially peripatetic, being Prince of Novgorod three times, Grand Prince of Kiev, and then Grand Prince of Vladimir. In 1272, Moscow was assigned to Prince Daniil Aleksandrovich, Nevsky's youngest son. Moscow was the least of Nevsky's holdings, and thus fit for a youngest son, but in the first year of his reign he – or rather his stewards, as he was only three years old at the time – began the construction of the wooden Church of the Transfiguration of the Saviour. More than a mark of piety, this would also have been an expression of confidence in Moscow's future – and confirmation that the Daniiloviches, the bloodline he would found, was here to stay.

But not without problems. This was the time of Mongol rule. Batu Khan's invading forces swept through Russia in their seemingly unstoppable conquests in 1237–42. Moscow was not a particular target then, but Grand Prince Yuri II of Vladimir-Suzdal had sent his sons Vsevolod and Vladimir to fight in the defence of Kolomna in January 1238. It was a bloody defeat, and the surviving Russians scattered, Vladimir ending up in Moscow. The locals, recognizing a hopeless cause when they saw one, apparently largely fled the town. (At least according to the Novgorod Chronicle, a source often happy to cast shade on its rival city, Moscow.) A small Mongol force duly took it, and Prince Vladimir too, after a short siege. Moscow suffered some damage, especially to its wall, but essentially survived the initial invasion in rather better shape than many other towns and cities of the Rus'.

Nonetheless, it would soon fall foul of subsequent struggles as the Golden Horde sought to enforce its rule, and Russian princes working for the Mongols used them to settle old scores and expand their own territories. In 1293, an army under Tudan, brother of the Khan of the Golden Horde, was unleashed as a result of a disruptive power struggle between princes. His mission was terror, and he sacked and burned a string of Russian cities: Suzdal, Vladimir, Pereslavl-Zalessky, Kolomna, Murom – and Moscow. It fell after five days of siege, its prince and all its defenders killed, the town and its church virtually burned to the ground.

Nevertheless, it would all quickly be rebuilt, bigger and better than ever. The new walls were higher, more complex, and enclosed a larger area. In parts, they were doubled up, with a second, taller wall allowing defenders to rain spears and arrows on attackers who had managed to storm the first. The prince's *detinets*, his citadel, was now a substantial rectangular building with two turrets and a similarly expanded stockade, also encompassing a chapel.

Other cities had been hit harder in the invasion, and the trade routes on which Moscow sat were even busier than before, especially given the need to exchange goods for silver to pay the Mongols' tribute. When not reminding the Russians of their power with steel and fire, the Mongols were distant, but enlightened, rulers and commerce boomed. The princes of Moscow had also learned a bitter but valuable lesson, though. Nevsky had from the first sought to cooperate with the Mongols, and his descendants would take this further, rising to become amongst their most ruthlessly efficient agents. In the process, they became rich and powerful.

The rise of Moscow

In 1327, after rival city Tver joined a rebellion against the Golden Horde, Ivan I of Moscow offered the Khan his services in putting it down. At the head of a combined force of Russian and Mongol troops, Ivan crushed Tver, devastated its lands, and plundered its treasury. In one blow, he eliminated a competitor and won the Khan's favour. He was granted the title of Grand Prince, effectively recognition that the Golden Horde considered the princes of Moscow first among equals.

In a further sign of Moscow's rise, the head of the Russian Orthodox Church, Metropolitan Pyotr, had moved his residence there in 1325, setting up inside the inner walls of the *gorod*. The year after, the first stone was laid in the construction of the new Cathedral of the Dormition. This was the first stone church in Moscow, built close to the prince's palace: even at that stage, spiritual and secular power was forging an alliance. Ivan I acquired the nickname *Kalita*, 'Moneybags', for the wealth he accrued as the Mongols' enforcer and tax collector, and some of that he and his successors would invest in making Moscow a city fit for a Grand Prince. By 1339, new oak walls and towers had been built, made of oak trunks up to 70cm in diameter and 15m long, enclosing a wider swathe of land. Towers up to 13m high were set no more than an easy bowshot apart, and the old corner towers, where the Trinity and Secret Towers now stand, became gates, with new corner towers built further north and east.

This is really when the term kremlin appears to have come into general use, denoting a fortress inside a wider city, although only later would 'the Kremlin' automatically imply Moscow's. The Kremlin became the political, religious and economic centre: while a *podol* sprawled out beyond its walls, those who could afford to live within it, did. Through the 14th century, no

Apollinari Vasnetsov's interpretation of Grand Prince Ivan Kalita's wooden Kremlin. Note the log stockade outside the walls themselves, and the thriving river traffic, such an important part of the city's original rise. (Public domain)

THE RISE OF THE MUSCOVITE STATE

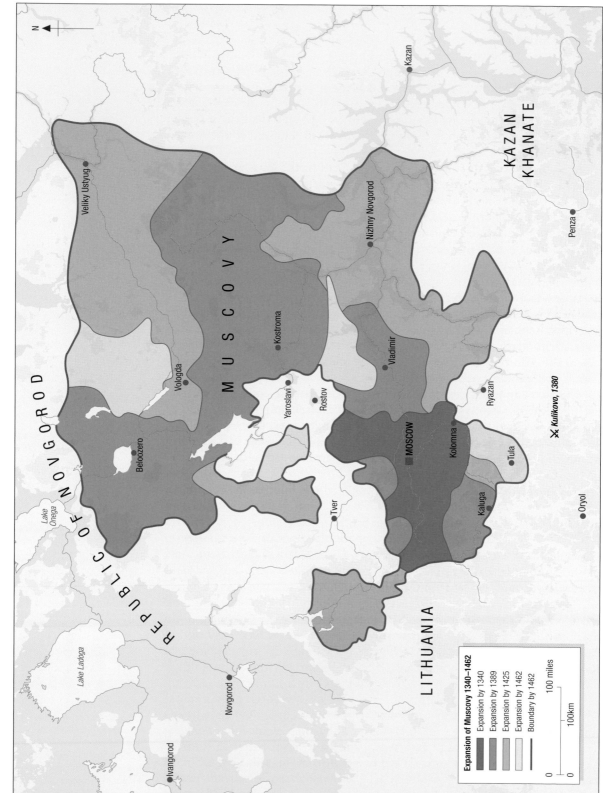

N

KAZAN KHANATE

Kazan

Penza

Veliky Ustyug

Nizhny Novgorod

M U S C O V Y

Kostroma

Vladimir

Vologda

Ryazan

Yaroslavl

Rostov

✕ *Kulikovo, 1380*

Belozero

MOSCOW

Kolomna

Tula

R E P U B L I C   O F   N O V G O R O D

Tver

Kaluga

Oryol

Lake
Onega

Lake Ladoga

L I T H U A N I A

Novgorod

Ivangorod

Expansion of Muscovy 1340–1462

Expansion by 1340
Expansion by 1389
Expansion by 1425
Expansion by 1462
Boundary by 1462

100 miles

100km

0
0

fewer than five monasteries and churches were built within the walls, as well as ever-more elaborate palaces. This was still a wooden fortress, though, with all the vulnerabilities that entailed. That situation could not be allowed to continue in what was becoming the capital of an increasingly unified Russia.

A WHITE-STONE FORTRESS

Ivan I's great-grandson, Dmitry I, has gone down in history as the victor of the battle of Kulikovo, the first major Russian triumph against the Golden Horde (though it would take another century to shake off the so-called 'Mongol Yoke'), winning himself the soubriquet *Donskoi*, 'of the Don'.[2] His reign (1359–89) saw the Kremlin rebuilt, besieged, razed and rebuilt again. For reasons of both security and prestige (and the perennial risk of fires, such as the one which raged through Moscow in 1365), he embarked on a major reconstruction. First, he replaced the wooden walls and towers with new defences made of an estimated 112,000 tonnes of white limestone quarried from nearby Myachkovo, hauled over 30km by sledge through the winter of 1366–67. Construction of what was the largest building project in Russia at the time, involving over 2,000 workers, began in the following spring.

A 16th-century illumination from the Russian Primary Chronicle showing the start of construction of Donskoi's stone Kremlin. (Public domain)

The new walls of the Kremlin stretched around 2km, and again pushed out the complex's bounds sufficiently that they entirely engulfed the old wooden walls, as well as the ditch across the remaining side of the fortress not flanked by river (a new one would later be dug further out). In such dangerous times, it was not feasible to leave the Kremlin undefended, so the older walls were only dismantled after the new ones had been built, and some remained – Moscow's defences would in due course come to resemble the classic *Matryoshka* nesting dolls, with walls ringing walls. The new walls, 2–3m thick, were first built to a height of just 2m all around, and then raised further until they reached a height of 4–7m, with crenelated tops. A combination of rectangular and circular towers anchored the walls and provided platforms for counter-siege artillery, such as stone- and javelin-throwing *arkballistas*, whose crossbows had a span of up to 2.5m, or the *brikol*, a catapult-style device that could fire one or a whole sheaf of javelins.

The building was complete in 1368 – just in time for the first of two sieges by Lithuanian forces under Prince Algirdas, the second being in 1370. Both times, the stone walls (and battle-hardened defenders) of the Kremlin weathered the Lithuanians' attacks. They were able to burn and loot the *podol* townships around it, but most of the population had either fled the city or sheltered inside the Kremlin. The 1368 siege lasted only three days: the attack had been launched in November, and Algirdas feared the onset of full winter, especially as

---

2   See CAM 332: *Kulikovo 1380: The battle that made Russia*

Vasnetsov's *The Defence of Moscow Against Tokhtamysh* shows the militia's muster against the Golden Horde in 1382; in the background, note the catapult mounted on one of the Kremlin's towers. (Public domain)

Muscovite forces were conducting raids of their own on Lithuanian-ruled territories. The 1370 attack was similarly more raid than full-blown siege, ending with a truce after Algirdas failed to catch the Muscovites by surprise. A chronicle recalled that Algirdas had come 'neither prepared for a lengthy campaign, nor with the weapons that could breach the white walls of Moscow'.

When the Kremlin fell in 1382, it was not to force of arms but cunning. In retaliation for Donskoi's victory at Kulikovo, the new Khan of the Golden Horde, Tokhtamysh, led a punitive expedition of 30,000 men that sent Dmitry fleeing to the subject city of Kostroma, and resulted in Moscow being encircled. The Kremlin again proved its strength, and despite three days of siege and attempted assault, Tokhtamysh's forces were unable to take it. This

Vasnetsov's depiction of the White-Stone Kremlin from the Borovitsky Gate side, before Tokhtamysh's attack of 1382. (Public domain)

was all the more impressive given that many of the defenders were not crack troops – Dmitry had taken his personal guard with him – but a ragtag militia of city-folk, stiffened by the remnants of his forces. Ultimately, it took subterfuge to end the siege. The princes of Suzdal, who had joined his side, persuaded the Muscovites that Tokhtamysh's feud was with Dmitry and not his people: if they just opened the gates in symbolic surrender, he would leave them be.

Beware the promises of conquerors. As soon as the gates were opened, Tokhtamysh's forces stormed into the Kremlin. They killed or enslaved all they could catch, sacked and burned whatever they could find. Probably tens of thousands were killed, or marched away into slavery. Nonetheless, when Dmitry returned, he put his money and his energy into rebuilding, stronger than ever. A good sacking does wonders for urban renewal: many of the old wooden buildings inside the walls and even outside them were rebuilt in stone, and the defences of the Kremlin extended.

The age of the gun

Dmitry's successors would continue to build, and as Moscow itself expanded, so did the Kremlin, its walls being periodically pushed out as they were rebuilt, higher and stronger than before, until the complex covered pretty much the full extent of the Borovitsky Hill. By the 15th century, however, the walls were beginning to show signs of serious wear, and the foundations were proving inadequate. They endured an earthquake in 1445, but the stresses it caused would lead to a series of small subsidences later. Small-scale repairs were a constant chore, gaps in the stone being shored up with wood, which represented an evident vulnerability: in 1451, Golden Horde raiders almost managed to get into the city through them.

There were well-founded concerns that the structure simply would not cope in the coming age of the cannon. Since the late 14th century, crude emplaced cannon such as the simple *tyufak* had been used by Moscow's garrison, first against Tokhtamysh's forces in 1382. Although the first Russian cannon foundry was only established – in Moscow – in 1475, by then they were already increasingly used also by attacking forces. Bronze-cast guns were used by both sides in the Ottoman siege of Constantinople in 1422 and the Russians, who maintained close diplomatic and trading links with what they called 'Tsargrad' – 'Emperor-City' – heard horrifying accounts of the power of these new weapons.

The need was for walls that suited the new realities of the gunpowder age. This meant thicker walls, angled berms to deflect cannon balls, and platforms and embrasures for defenders' guns. In 1462, the first major reconstruction project was carried out, with a section of wall between the Borovitsky Gate and the Sviblov Tower (later renamed the Vodovzvodnaya, or Water-Lifting Tower) at the 'tip' of the Kremlin, overlooking the confluence of the Moskva and Neglinnaya Rivers. It was, after all, highest and most visible to enemy artillery on the opposite banks of the river. This would, however, only highlight the problems with the existing structure; flaws in the foundations and constructions were literally pushing limestone blocks out of the walls. It was time for a comprehensive reconstruction, and that would be handled not by local construction entrepreneurs, largely self-taught in traditional methods, but a new wave of architect-builders from Italy, attracted to Moscow, well-versed in the latest military architecture from Europe.

A fistful of churches

Even in pagan times, the Kremlin was as much a site of religious devotion as secular power. The Orthodox Church was closely tied to the princes of Moscow since Metropolitan Pyotr's transfer of his See, and outside Moscow, monasteries were often fortified as strongpoints against the continuing threat of nomad raids. The Church was wealthy in its own right, with lands and serfs and taxes of its own, but church-building was, for the princes and the boyars, as much a way to demonstrate their wealth as their piety. The Moscow Kremlin was a place of constant construction and reconstruction, as churches, monasteries, belltowers and chapels were added, expanded and rebuilt. In particular, Ivan III built two white-walled and golden-domed cathedrals: the Cathedral of the Assumption (or Dormition), on the site of Daniil's original wooden church, and the Cathedral of the Annunciation, built on the crest of the hill, at the south end of what was now being called the *Sobornaya Ploshchad'* (Cathedral Square), as the prince's private chapel.

In the 16th century, as Vasnetsov's famous representation shows, the red-brick walls of Ivan III's Kremlin had been completed, and while many of the buildings inside the complex were still wood, they were increasingly being replaced with stone and brick mansions and churches, with the renovated Cathedral of the Assumption dominating the centre. (Public domain)

RED-BRICK KREMLIN

In 1485, Ivan III, Ivan the Great, embarked on an ambitious programme to rebuild the Kremlin, inside and out.[3] His line had effectively reunited most of Russia under their rule and it was time to build a capital reflecting both its new power and the threats of the age. Having married Sofia Paleologue, a princess of the now-defunct Byzantine imperial line, he was eager to assert his claim to be an emperor in his own right – he was the first Russian ruler to call himself Tsar, emperor, rather than Grand Prince – and position Moscow as

the natural successor to 'Tsargrad', calling it the 'Third Rome' and adopting Byzantium's double-headed eagle symbol. He wanted grandeur and security; Paleologue, wanted elegance and sophistication. To get them both, they sent their agents shopping in Italy.

After all, Italian architects had already made a name for themselves in Russia, and the Renaissance was in full bloom. Although the consensus was that Germans were marginally better at making cannon, otherwise Italians were deemed the best architects and engineers, most up-to-date in

[3] See FOR 39: *Russian Fortresses 1480–1682*

C THE BRICK KREMLIN, c. 1640

Before the decision in 1680 to paint the walls and towers white again to symbolize purity, Ivan III's red-brick fortress made a particularly vivid spectacle in the snows of a Russian winter. Here viewed from the east, the scale of the complex is especially visible. The flooded Aleviz Ditch makes for an imposing moat, faced with crenelated brick walls, bridged at the Beklemishevskaya, Konstantino-Yeleninskaya, Spasskaya, Nikolskaya and Corner Arsenal Towers, the first and last of which also connect to the Kitay-Gorod walls. Note the additional wall along the bank of the Moskva, with the *otvodnaya strelnitsa* bastion connecting it to the Secret Tower (1). The Petrovskaya Tower (2), destroyed by Polish artillery fire in 1612, is finally completing reconstruction. A force of *Streltsy* is heading into Kitay-Gorod from the Spassky Gate (3). The recently built Heraldic Tower (4) is the only one of the main towers here not to survive until today. Note the new water-wheel at the Vodovzvodnaya Tower (5).

their understanding of how changes in military technology, from gunpowder weapons to siegecraft, were changing fortress design. Under the supervision of Italian architects such as Marco Ruffo and Pietro Solari, the whole Kremlin was rebuilt.

Ivan's Italians

Ivan III's representatives recruited several leading Italian architects, as well as the craftsmen to serve them. Some would return home afterwards, but others were less fortunate. One was Ridolfo 'Aristotele' Fioravanti, from Bologna. He was engaged by Ivan's agent, Semyon Tolbuzin, on a salary of ten roubles a month, generous even for a recognized master. He came to Moscow in 1475 with his son Andrea. There are tales that he was imprisoned by Ivan when he later wanted to return to Italy, but the truth is that he was also an accomplished military engineer and cannon-maker, so instead he seems to have been offered the choice between dungeon or continued service to Moscow. Unsurprisingly, he chose the latter, and played a role in subsequent campaigns against Novgorod (1477–78), Kazan (1482) and Tver (1485), dying in 1486.

Marco Ruffo from Milan was known in Moscow as Marko Fryazin – *Fryazin*, 'Frank', being a generic Russian term for any Northern Italian – and spent a decade there, 1485–95, working on the Kremlin walls and several of its towers, as well as the Chamber of Facets. Pietro Antonio Solari was predictably also known as Pyotr Fryazin.

These two made it back home, but other 'Fryazins' did not, including Aloisio da Carezano from Milan, Aleviz Fryazin to the Russians, a contemporary with a particular expertise in hydraulic architecture – and so the name is now an established Russian surname, and around this time an estate called Fryazino was set up, 25km north-east of Moscow.

The crumbling limestone walls and towers, built for an age of archers and catapults, were dismantled or demolished (often, the rubble was used for the new foundations), and a new set of defences built in a ten-year project running from 1485 to 1495. In the process, the walls of the Kremlin were pushed back to enclose an area of 27.5 hectares (68 acres, or almost 39 football pitches), close to its present shape and size. The new battlements were made of hard, fired red brick, at once resilient and regular, built around a core of cemented limestone rubble. Each large brick weighed up to 8kg. The Kremlin became a red-brick fortress.

The Italian architects brought their vernacular with them, especially reminiscent of Verona's 14th-century Castelvecchio and Milan's 15th-century Castello Sforzesco. The Kremlin's chest-height battlements have the distinctive swallowtail crenelation, known as the Ghibelline, with deep V-shaped notches in the tops of the merlons, reminiscent of the Milanese fortress. As well as providing good cover to defenders (who also could cover the gaps between with wooden shields), it is an elegant design. That presumably appealed to Ivan's desire to build not just a strong fastness but also an expression of Muscovite authority.

This picture of the changing of the guard at the Tomb of the Unknown Soldier clearly shows not just the height of the walls but also the swallowtail merlons. (Vladimir Gerdo\TASS via Getty Images)

Depending on the underlying terrain, the walls – which despite periodic destruction, neglect and reconstruction, are essentially those of today – were between 5m and 19m high and 3.5–6.5m thick, with a total length of 2.2km. On the outside, they presented a smooth face to make scaling them harder, but on the inside they featured arched niches to both lighten yet also strengthen them.

Embrasures with hinged wooden covers were built along the lower parts of the wall, allowing artillery to fire on attackers from cover, while gun platforms were also incorporated into the flat roofs of many towers (then covered by conical or pyramidal wooden superstructures). Arched passages ran through the wall between some towers, although they largely ended up choked with construction debris. There were also secret access points and passages under the walls, both to allow covert entry or exit from the Kremlin (one was close to the Grand-Ducal Palace), and to facilitate counter-mining operations if a besieger tried to dig tunnels of their own under the walls.

The Kolomna kremlin was built in 1525, modelled on Moscow's, and this stretch of surviving walls shows the brickwork, including the arched construction on the inside face. (Author's collection)

The so-called Aleviz Ditch was dug in 1508–16 under the supervision of da Carezano: 8m deep and 36m across at its widest point, it was faced with brick and stone and filled with water from the Neglinnaya. Three dams along the lower reaches of the Neglinnaya were built for both flood control and industrial purposes, with water mills providing power for the Cannon Yard and the Royal Mint inside the Kremlin, as well as threshing and grinding grain. The Kremlin was at last surrounded by water.

Five gates, set in sturdy towers, provided the only points of entry and egress, with bridges across either the Neglinnaya or the Aleviz Ditch. In some cases, the bridges were simple wooden affairs – although they were soon replaced with arched stone ones – but in each case an *otvodnaya strelnitsa*, or 'diversionary tower', was built at the other end of the bridge for extra security. Typically, the main town would mount a drawbridge and wrought-iron portcullises sealed in the gatehouses. A further 14 towers studded the walls, as detailed in the section 'Twenty Towers'.

Ivan III also decreed that, to minimize the risk of fire, all buildings within ten *sazhen*s of the Kremlin wall – a *sazhen* was an archaic Russian measure some 7ft or 2.13m in length – were demolished, to give a clear zone more than 20m deep around them. In practice, the sprawl of stalls and huts would periodically encroach into this perimeter, only to be pushed back.

The Kremlin inside the walls went through almost as dramatic a reconstruction. Fioravanti and Ruffo built the new Grand-Ducal Palace, a project that would take even longer than the walls, being started in 1485 and only being completed in 1514. They also built the stunning Chamber of Facets, the princely banqueting hall, that later became the Palace of Facets when the rest of the building was demolished. On its southern facade is the Red Porch, a stone staircase decorated with stylized lions, down which generations of tsars would ceremonially process on their way to the Cathedral of the Dormition for coronation. Lamberti Aloisio da Mantagnana (known as Aloisio the New, Aleviz Novy) built the new Cathedral of the Archangel, in whose crypt generations of tsars would be buried.

Ivan the Terrible's Kremlin

By the time Ivan IV became the first monarch actually to be crowned as Tsar in 1547, the redefinition of the Kremlin was essentially complete. Now known more widely as Ivan the Terrible – although his soubriquet *Grozny* is better translated as Formidable or Awesome – his was a reign of two halves. While always brooding and bloodthirsty, his early reign was also one of serious state-building. He laid the foundations for the Russian bureaucratic system and standing army and finally extended Moscow's rule south over the Khanates of Kazan and Astrakhan. Later, he sank into murderous and erratic paranoia and all but ripped that state apart, leading after his death to the extended period of unrest, invasion and civil war called the Time of Troubles.

This was all reflected in the Kremlin. By the mid-16th century, the contours of the modern Kremlin were essentially set. The main streets inside the walls were expanded and later cobbled: Spasskaya, Nikolskaya and Chudovskaya. Cathedral Square was the heart of this complex, and what was now the Tsar's Palace was regularly expanded and remodelled. Military triumphs were celebrated in the very fabric of the Kremlin. The domes on the Annunciation Cathedral were increased to nine and these, along with those on the Assumption Cathedral, were gilded with gold seized from old enemy Kazan, when Ivan the Terrible conquered the city in 1552.

The Ivan the Great Belltower on the eastern side of Cathedral Square was originally 60m tall, but in 1600 it was raised to fully 81m, which meant that for almost four centuries it would remain the tallest building in Russia. In part this was for prestige but it also had a practical significance, as it was also used as a watchtower, from which approaching invaders could be spotted – but also potential enemies closer to hand could be observed.

The Red Porch remained a fixture in major ceremonies through to the end of tsarism. Here Alexander II descends its steps on his way to his coronation in 1856. (Public domain)

After all, this was a time of growing civil turmoil, as the tsar had to fear not only the Moscow mob, but also his own nobility. Much of the Kremlin, especially north of Cathedral Square, was occupied still by the estates and mansions of lesser princes, boyars, rich merchants and clergy. Political and economic struggles between powerful houses could often erupt into violence. More to the point, as Ivan's state of mind decayed, he began to see plots in every shadow. It was said that his agents would watch the movements of people from one *dvor* to another from the vantage point of the belltower for hints of conspiracies being hatched against the crown.

Ivan played favourites and punished real or suspected enemies, and many of these Kremlin estates were seized and redistributed to his cronies, or in some cases simply demolished. What had for centuries been a city within a city, shared between the grand prince and his aristocracy, was increasingly becoming simply a stronghold of the tsars, although it would take the best part of a century for this process to be completed.

As part of this process, Ivan created Russia's first standing army, the *Streltsy* ('Shooters'), to free him of dependence on the feudal levies and personal entourages of the aristocracy. As their name suggests, the *Streltsy* were infantry armed with *pischal*s, arquebuses, an innovation for its day, as well as the distinctive crescent-bladed poleaxe known as a *berdysh*. Recruited from the urban free – farmers, labourers and craftsmen – they were paid a meagre salary of 4 roubles a year, but on top of that allowed to practise their trades when not on duty or in the field and were granted tax dispensations. They settled in adjacent neighbourhoods of Moscow, especially Zamoskvorechie ('Across the Moskva River'), but assumed duties throughout the city, patrolling the streets and fighting fires. They also took over responsibility for guarding the Kremlin, on rotating week-long assignment.

A fine study from the 19th century of the Ivan the Great Belltower, and its belfry to the side. (Public domain)

A 19th-century engraving of the mighty *Tsar Pushka*, or Tsar Cannon. Cast in bronze in 1586 in the Kremlin's Cannon Yard, this 40-ton brute had an 89cm calibre and could fire a 1-ton cannonball. However, it never saw action, although in 1591 it was emplaced in Kitay-Gorod to protect the main Kremlin gates and the crossing over the Moskva when Crimean Khan Kazy-Girey II was threatening the city. Having long symbolically guarded the Spassky Gates, it now sits by the belfry of the Ivan the Great Belltower, on the opposite side from the Tsar Bell. (Public domain)

A 1613 engraving showing *Streltsy* in Red Square, bearing their standard weapons, a sabre, a *pischal* arquebus and a *berdysh* pole axe; note the cartridges hanging from their sashes. (Public domain)

Matryoshka Moscow

Many of Moscow's neighbourhoods were encircled by *tyn*s, simple wooden stockades, some with proper gates, others simply barricaded when raiders were near. Over the next few decades, though, the city acquired concentric city walls that made it increasingly defensible and, in the process, took the onus of security off the Kremlin itself.

The first to be walled was the *posad*, or mercantile quarter, adjacent to the Kremlin known as Kitay-Gorod (technically 'Chinatown', but actually deriving from *kita*, an old term for braiding and basket-work, reflecting the old practice of building walls of earth-filled basketry). An increasingly prosperous trading district, in 1394 what was then called the *Veliky Posad* (the Great *Posad*) had been encircled by a ditch except for the side occupied by the Kremlin. This ditch was later reinforced with a wall, firstly of those woven wood compartments packed with earth, eventually replaced by a log stockade. However, in 1535, regent Yelena Glinskaya decreed the construction of a wall. Petrok Maly spent three years building a solid brick curtain wall that enclosed 63 hectares next to the Kremlin. It began at the Kremlin's Beklemishevskaya Tower, stretched along the Moskva River, and in due course returned to the Kremlin's Corner Arsenal Tower. The total length of this wall was 2.6km, and it was lower, but wider, than the Kremlin's battlements, generally around 6m high but fully 4m wide, such that a cart could be driven along

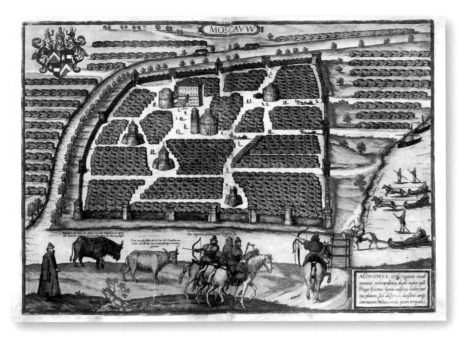

The engraved map of the Kremlin by Sigismund von Herberstein, published in 1556 but based on his time there between 1517 and 1526, is a little inaccurate and rudimentary but does evoke the times and also the degree to which this was still a walled township within a city. (Public domain)

its wall-walk. The wall was surmounted by crenelations (albeit plain ones compared with the Kremlin's pointed merlons) and essentially built for solidity rather than elegance. It had six gate-towers and 13 other towers. They typically had three fighting floors with loopholes and cannon platforms at the top. The towers' basements housed magazines, and many also had so-called *slukh*s, 'hearings' or 'rumours': underground chambers sheathed in sheet copper, from which defenders could listen out for enemy tunnelling.

In 1586, to minimize the threat from further raids, an even more extensive wall began being built, around the whole heart of Moscow, including both the Kremlin and Kitay-Gorod. Only completed in 1593, the wall was some 10km (6.2 miles) long, with 11 gates and fully 28 towers. It was a composite: a central well filled with rubble and lime concrete, inside two brick walls. Some 5–8m in height and up to 4.5m wide, it was topped with swallowtail merlon battlements and a wall-walk. Much of the enclosed area was packed with wooden houses, shops, warehouses and churches, but there were many estates of boyars and nobles, whose land was known as 'white' because it was exempt from the land taxes levied on the 'black' properties of those not in direct tsarist service. Whether for this reason, or because of the whitewashed appearance of the wall, this area came to be known as *Bely Gorod* or White City. In the late 18th century, the walls were dismantled, replaced by the wide roads of the Boulevard Ring.

Most distinctive of the White City fortifications was the Semiverkhaya or Seven-Headed Tower on the space today occupied by the Cathedral of Christ the Saviour. A hexagonal tower, 25m tall, it was topped with seven pyramidal turrets and a crenelated gun platform. Its very strength would be its undoing. In 1611, when Russian

This picture shows the sheer bulk of the Corner Arsenal Tower, a fortification in its own right, 60m tall with 4m-thick walls, that now houses elements of the Kremlin Guard. It also anchored one end of the Kitay-Gorod walls, until their destruction. (Author's collection)

Vasnetskov's depiction of the Skorodom's wooden fortifications along the Yauza River underlines how, while not of the same scale as the brick-and-stone inner defences, it was nonetheless a credible outer rampart against nomad raids. (Public domain)

forces were recapturing Moscow from the Poles, several times they tried to dislodge the Polish garrison with no success. Eventually, having learned from a deserter about the location of a powder magazine in the base of the tower, they sent a flurry of fire-arrows at the relevant loopholes and managed to ignite it, blasting a hole in the wall and bringing down several floors. The tower was rebuilt, but later had to be demolished.

In 1591, in response to another raid, by Crimean Khan Kazy-Girey II, Tsar Boris Godunov ordered the urgent creation of an even wider ring wall around the city as a whole, including scattered outer farms. This was known as the *Derevyanny Gorod*, Wooden City, or more usually *Skorodom*, 'Quickly Built', because it was largely completed in a year. While this was in part because of the extensive use of serfs, it also reflected the much simpler nature of the defences: a 10–16m-wide ditch backed by an earthen berm topped with a 6m-tall wooden wall of oak logs. It stretched some 23km (over 14 miles), with 12 gate-towers and 45 other towers, mostly rectangular wooden structures typically mounting 4–6 cannon apiece.

Largely burned down by the Poles in 1611, it was later rebuilt before being replaced in 1638–41 by the *Zemlyannoy Val*, the Earthern Rampart. This largely followed the line of the *Skorodom*, but extended further to include a mix of *slobodas* – villages or *posad*s whose inhabitants owed the tsar service instead of taxes – in the Zamoskvorechye neighbourhood. This was built of wooden walls around an earth core raised atop an earth rampart behind a ditch. It had 11 gates and 57 towers. Only two of the gatehouses, Serpukhov and Kaluga, were built of stone, as they were deemed at greatest risk from Tatar raids, with the wooden Sretensky Gates being replaced by stone ones in the 1690s. Again, these walls were demolished in the late 18th century – a few gates survived through to the early 20th – and today's Garden Ring roads trace its old shape.

1571: fire

These were dangerous times, after all, and even Moscow was not secure. The Crimean Tatars continued periodically to raid deep into Russian territory, with the support of the Ottoman Empire, for whom they were convenient proxies. At other times, it was the Khanate of Kazan, or the Lithuanians, or the Swedes, or all of them, who encouraged the Crimeans in their expeditions of slave-taking, looting, plunder and general mayhem, as it forced Moscow to devote effort and manpower into trying to defend against them. In 1571, however, a much larger than usual force of Crimean Tatars, backed by Turkish regulars, bypassed Russian defensive fortifications, flanked and routed a small field force, and headed straight for Moscow.

The attackers pillaged the towns and villages around Moscow, and then advanced on the city. The Crimean Khan, Devlet-Giray, ordered the outer

MOSCOW'S WALLS

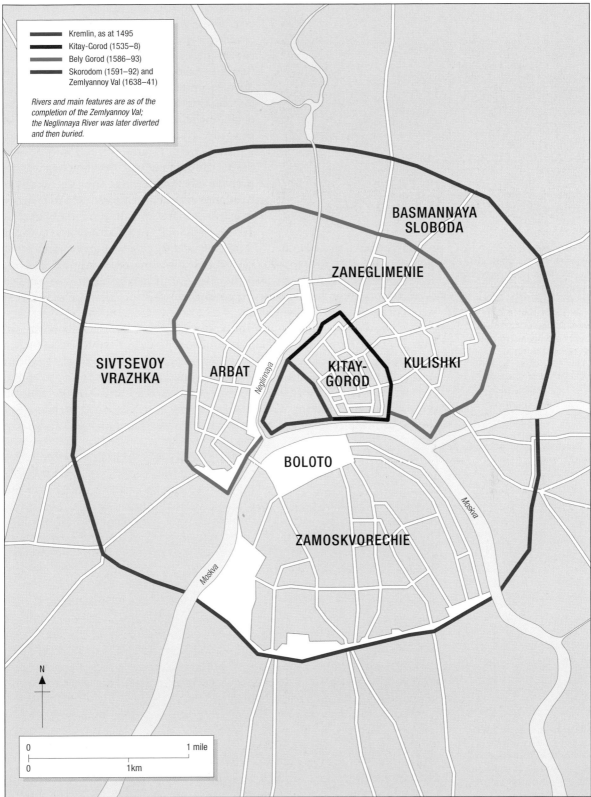

Kremlin, as at 1495
Kitay-Gorod (1535–8)
Bely Gorod (1586–93)
Skorodom (1591–92) and
Zemlyannoy Val (1638–41)

Rivers and main features are as of the completion of the Zemlyannoy Val; the Neglinnaya River was later diverted and then buried.

BASMANNAYA
SLOBODA

ZANEGLIMENIE

SIVTSEVOY
VRAZHKA

ARBAT

KITAY-
GOROD

KULISHKI

Neglinnaya

BOLOTO

ZAMOSKVORECHIE

Moskva

Moskva

N

0   1 mile
0   1km

Fyodor Alekseyev's representation of the Nikolsky Gates in the Kitay-Gorod walls; note the familiar plan of the tower, evocative of Kremlin towers with its tiled, multi-stage roof, as well as the overhang with machicolations. (Public domain)

suburbs put to the torch and strong winds quickly drove the fire into the centre of the city. Those who had not already fled or who could not get into the Kremlin, flocked to the northern gates of Kitay-Gorod, which became bottlenecks where people died crushed under the feet of their fellows. As city folk interpenetrated the lines of the defending troops, the latter panicked or lost their order, joining the headlong flight.

The Kremlin gates were closed against the mob, but the winds blew burning embers over the moats and walls, causing a series of fires inside the complex. The powder magazine for the guns in the First Nameless Tower exploded, but fortunately a wider conflagration was contained. Nonetheless, the city was devastated, and anywhere from 20,000 to 80,000 died that day. In a desperate bid to avert disease, corpses were flung into the rivers, and according to the English explorer and envoy Jerome Horsey, writing in 1573, it took more than a year for all of them to be washed away.

Ivan would avoid the city for the next few years, both out of superstition and also because his palaces had been burned. Parts of the Kremlin had to be rebuilt, but fortunately for the *Streltsy*, their source of weapons survived. After all, most of their guns were actually made in the Kremlin. The original Armoury (*Oruzheinaya palata*) was established in 1508 on the basis of the existing Treasury (*Kazenny dvor*) as both a repository for the princely regalia and other especially valuable items and also a site

This impression of the 16th-century Pushechny Dvor, or Cannon Yard, is a reminder of its former role as a source of weapons for the tsar's armies. (Public domain)

for making and storing weapons, alongside the Cannon Yard. It ensured that the *Streltsy* were among the best-armed fighting men in Russia, and also that there was a substantial stock of weapons inside the Kremlin walls in case of a rising or an attempted boyar coup. Originally taking up just two floors of a three-storey, pyramid-roofed building next to the Trinity Gate, after a serious fire in 1547 it extended to the rest of the building. In the 17th century, before Peter the Great moved to his new city of St Petersburg in 1713, it assumed the role of the army's quartermasters, keeping the military not just armed but also fed and uniformed, as Russia began to build a European-style force. However, it never lost its role as a manufactory, the working day running from dawn to dusk, the air around the building heavy with the smoke of the forges and ringing with the din of hammer on anvil.

Much of this construction is visible in the first reliable maps of the Kremlin at our disposal. Sigismund von Herberstein was a diplomat working for the court of the Holy Roman Empire, twice sent on missions to Moscow, in 1517 and 1526. These missions were lengthy (nine months in the first instance) and von Herberstein was a keen amateur cartographer, so he compiled an extensive plan of the Kremlin. Later, Dutch cartographer Gerrits Hessel produced his own map of 'Kremlenagrad'. Another visitor was the Persian diplomat Oruj Bek Bayat, who travelled with an embassy to Moscow in 1599 and was stuck for five months of winter because of bad weather. Nonetheless, he was impressed: 'houses in the Kremlin were built in the style of Italian architects and decorated with beautiful ornaments. The king's palace is especially beautiful.' And this was from a cosmopolitan figure from Constantinople (and who would later be described as the 'Don Juan of Persia'). Moscow and the Kremlin had come far from their early beginnings as a crude stockade in the woods.

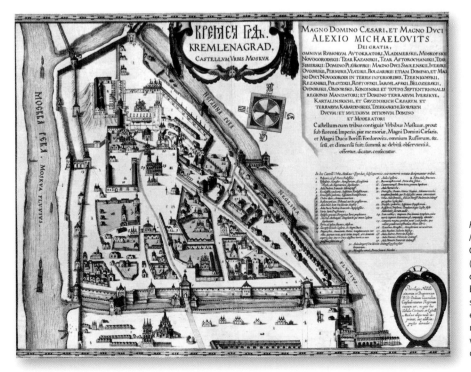

Kremlenagrad Castellum Urbis Moskvae, the 'Kremlenagrad Castle of the City of Moscow' (1663) was one of the first detailed maps of the fortress, by Gerrits Hessel. It clearly shows the *dvor*s, the enclosed estates of boyars and rich merchants that remained within the walls. (Public domain)

TIMES OF TROUBLES

The 17th century saw new palaces and churches added to the existing line-up as the new Romanov dynasty made its own mark on the Kremlin. The main visual change was the addition of elaborate, fluted turrets decorated with coloured tiles atop the Kremlin towers, giving them the distinctive silhouette still visible today. It is ironic that it did not change more, though, given the degree to which this would be a turbulent century, the Kremlin seeing coups, regicide, risings and brief Polish domination.

A Polish fortress (briefly)

The death of sickly Tsar Fyodor I in 1598 left no real heirs within the Ryurikid bloodline. The result was a series of coups, civil wars and succession crises that coincided with famine (1601–03) and foreign invasion. King Sigismund III of Poland took advantage of the Time of Troubles to back a contender to the throne, who claimed to be the rightful heir, Dmitry, who had actually died in 1591. The 'False Dmitry' led a small army into Russia in 1604, and on the unexpected death of Tsar Boris Godunov in 1605, many of the boyars hailed him tsar. However, Dmitry never had much real support, and his close links with the Catholic Poles generated considerable suspicion. In 1606, boyars under Vasily Shuisky whipped up the mob against him and stormed the Kremlin, where the continued presence of commonwealth troops had angered the Russian garrison to the point that they stood by. Dmitry was killed, his cremated ashes later shot from a cannon in the direction of Poland.

Klavdy Lebedev's *The entry of the troops of False Dmitry I into Moscow on 20 June 1605* clearly shows the original wooden pyramidal roofs over the red-brick towers, as well as the crenelated facing walls of the Aleviz Ditch. (Public domain)

Shuisky was duly crowned Vasili IV, but he was a better plotter than monarch. In 1607, a second 'False Dmitry' appeared at the head of an army of Polish troops and mercenaries, and in 1610 Vasili IV was forced to taste his own medicine. His boyars deposed him, deciding a negotiated surrender was better than unconditional conquest. A Polish-Lithuanian army entered Moscow and Polish Crown Prince Wladyslaw IV was hailed as the new tsar. This was understandably seen as treason by many, especially as a Polish-Lithuanian garrison under Colonel Alexander Gonsiewski then occupied the Kremlin, in defiance of previous undertakings. Tensions between the Orthodox Russians and the Catholic garrison were inevitable, as the latter treated Moscow as a conquered city.

Incidents accumulated. A drunken Polish sentry shot at the icon of the Virgin Mary over the Kremlin's Nikolsky Gate, and although Gonsiewski punished him ruthlessly, having his hands cut off and nailed below the icon, this did little to appease the Muscovites. Then, an argument between a market seller and a Polish soldier escalated into a brawl and then a massacre, with 15 Muscovites killed. In January 1611, Hermogenes, Patriarch of Moscow and All the Russias, circulated a letter despairing 'how your Fatherland is being plundered, how they defile holy icons and churches, how innocent blood is being shed'. Although there was considerable sympathy for Hermogenes' call to arms in Moscow, it was difficult to organize under the Poles' direct gaze. Instead, Prokopy Lyapunov, the *voivode* (governor) of nearby Ryazan, was inspired to organize a ragtag force that called itself the First People's Militia.

In March, it moved on Moscow. The Poles were caught by surprise, not having even mounted all their cannon on the Kremlin walls. As church bells were rung across the city, Muscovites joined the attack. At first, momentum was with the Russians, but Gonsiewski commanded a force of 5,000 commonwealth veterans, and another 2,000 German mercenaries. The defenders' experience, organization and discipline began to count, and they had the formidable defences of the Kremlin on which to rely. With little in the way of heavy artillery or trained engineers, the attackers lost their momentum. The choice seemed to be between a lengthy siege, risking that commonwealth relief forces would arrive in time to lift it, or a bloody storming of the walls of Kitay-Gorod, followed by an even more dangerous direct assault on the Kremlin. This was a time for decisive leadership and tactical acumen; instead, the First People's Militia fell victim to faction-fighting. Polish agents successfully persuaded the Cossack contingents through a forged letter that Lyapunov planned to betray them. He was summoned to a council of Cossack leaders and summarily hacked to death.

The First People's Militia began to fall apart. The commonwealth forces began to launch sallies from their fortified base, and if not reassert control over the city, at least break up any concentrations of enemy forces. However, a Second People's Militia soon emerged in Nizhny Novgorod, east of Moscow. Kuzma Minin, a merchant, proved a very capable organizer, while his collaborator Prince Dmitry Pozharsky (who had participated in the first assault) was an effective and charismatic commander. Having learned the lessons of the First People's Militia, they made a point of recruiting siege engineers, and also maintaining a more unified command structure.

In August 1612, they attacked a large cavalry force under Hetman Jan Karol Chodkiewicz bringing reinforcement and supplies to the garrison.

An idealized mural facing the Kremlin commemorates Prince Pozharsky and Kuzma Minin, leaders of the Second People's Militia that freed Moscow of Polish-Lithuanian forces in 1612. (Author's collection)

After three days of fighting, Chodkiewicz was forced to withdraw when Cossacks who had been with the First People's Militia joined the fray. The story is that this was only after the cellarer of the wealthy Trinity-Sergius Monastery promised to pay them from the monastic treasury.

The commonwealth garrison was now under Mikolai Strus. Gonsiewski had left that summer, taking with him the remainder of the Kremlin treasury and a regiment of battle-hardened commonwealth troops to guard them. These had been replaced with a regiment of Hungarian infantry, who proved competent but less motivated. They still held central Moscow, though, and the conflict settled down into a siege. Within a month, the Russians had retaken Kitay-Gorod, but the Kremlin remained inviolate. Polish cannon made attempts to launch assaults against the walls suicidal, and the lightly armed Cossack cavalry who made up perhaps a third of the Russian forces were of little value in this kind of fighting. The garrison had ample powder and shot – but not food. Without Chodkiewicz's supplies, and unable to forage outside the Kremlin's walls, they were going hungry. First they ate their horses, then any dogs, cats or even rats they could find. They chewed on leather belts and, according to possibly exaggerated accounts, even dug up decaying corpses in a desperate quest for food.

At the end of September, Pozharsky offered an honourable surrender, and many Russian collaborators who had been bottled up inside the Kremlin took the opportunity to flee. However, as it became clear that no commonwealth forces were coming to relieve them, and as German and Hungarian soldiers began quietly to risk night-time desertion, Strus realized he was out of options. In November, he duly surrendered, and, to the ringing of bells, Pozharsky, his forces, and jubilant Muscovites flocked back into the Kremlin. On hearing the news, Sigismund abandoned his dreams of empire and returned to Poland.

1682: rising

No one could fail to notice that the *Streltsy* had not distinguished themselves in the Time of Troubles, and it was a militia that drove the Polish-Lithuanian

D   MIKHAIL ROMANOV'S KREMLIN

The end of the Time of Troubles saw 17-year-old Mikhail Romanov crowned as tsar and start a new dynasty in 1613. The Kremlin was in poor condition, and he had to wait for weeks at the Troitsa Monastery outside Moscow before the royal palace was fit for his arrival. Here, in July 1613, the tsar-to-be Mikhail is ceremonially arriving at the Spassky Gates. As custom dictated,

he was approaching on foot, bare-headed. He is preceded by the icon of the Mother of God, and followed by a gaggle of boyars, the commander of an Order of *Streltsy*, and Mikhail's page, leading his horse. Although efforts have been made to make some repairs, the Kremlin still shows the ravages of Polish-Lithuanian occupation and the recent campaign to expel them.

Re-enactors in Moscow playing the role of *Streltsy:* the creation of a standing force of musketeers was a significant step forward for the consolidation of the tsar's power, but would also contribute to later palace intrigue and violent revolt. (Anton Novoderezhkin\TASS via Getty Images)

forces out of Moscow. They had increasingly lost their martial edge, becoming a hereditary force with aspirations to becoming kingmakers – or rather tsarmakers. Ever-more unruly, they sometimes sided with the mob (such as during the 1662 Copper Coin Riot against the issue of new coins, widely seen as a devaluation of the currency), and were often party to violent palace intrigues. One such emerged with the death of Tsar Fyodor III in 1682, leaving no adult heir. Two boyar families, the Miloslavskies and the Naryshkins, had rival claims on the throne and the Moscow *Strelets* regiments, believing rumours that the Naryshkins had had one of the young contenders to the throne strangled, declared for the Miloslavskies.

On 11 May, *Streltsy* conspirators disarmed loyalist commanders and seized the Kremlin. There followed a bloodbath. The *Streltsy* stormed through the complex, looting and lynching Naryshkin partisans. Prince General Grigory Romodanovsky was thrown down the staircase of the Red Porch onto mutineers' pikes. Artamon Matveyev, who had once headed the Strelets Office, was hacked to pieces. After days of violence, the young half-brothers Ivan and Peter were declared 'co-tsars', with the Miloslavskies' Sophia Alekseyevna as regent.

Capital no more

Peter – who would later be known as Peter the Great – never forgot the terror of those days and would eventually suppress the *Streltsy* and replace them with a European-style army. He would also never see Moscow in the same light again. With his accession to the throne in his own right in 1682, the city and the Kremlin began to lose their old prominence. (The Kremlin had already lost its distinctive colour: from 1680, its walls and towers were whitewashed to evoke the old limestone walls and spiritual purity.)

At first, Peter spent most of his time at his country estate of Preobrazhenskoye, then he embarked on the ambitious project of building a

new capital in the north. St Petersburg was formally inaugurated in 1703 and became the national capital in 1713. The Kremlin remained a royal residence, but began to be seen as an old-fashioned relic compared with the graceful new palaces of St Petersburg. Besides which, in 1701 a terrible fire had ripped through the Kremlin, prompting Peter to decree that no more wooden buildings could be built inside its walls.

At the height of the Great Northern War, there was a fear of Swedish invasion. This led to a flurry of activity refurbishing the Kremlin's defences, with new firing positions to accommodate larger modern guns, and expanded powder magazines to match. Linear outworks known as *bolverk*s (from the imported word bulwark) were hurriedly built along the old moat, which had long been drained. The Neglinnaya River itself was diverted to a new channel away from the western wall of the Kremlin. Yet these fears as quickly subsided with victory at Poltava in 1708, and increasingly the emphasis was placed on elegant display over defensive capability. The *bolverk*s were dismantled, although the wider firing stations in the towers and the firing embrasures in the walls that had already been built remained.

In 1768, to make room for a new palace in the latest classicist style – all the rage in St Petersburg – a stretch of the Kremlin wall to the south was even demolished, along with the Tainitskaya and First Nameless Towers. In 1775, this project was cancelled on budgetary grounds, and the wall and towers rebuilt, largely with the original bricks. Increasingly, though, a lack of funds to keep the Kremlin properly maintained was taking its toll. Meanwhile, the Neglinnaya River was built over, enclosed into a somewhat rough-and-ready stone tunnel, into which drained runoff water and sewage alike. In 1817–19, this would be upgraded to a proper brick-vaulted tunnel extending three kilometres, clearing the area that would later become the Alexandrovsky Gardens.

It seemed that every new monarch had their own ideas for the beautification of the Kremlin,

and every grand plan ended up delayed by financial reasons and then overtaken by events. The one major construction project which did go ahead was the erection of a new Senate building, completed in 1787. To accommodate this, the last private estates still surviving inside the Kremlin were cleared out. It may not have been Russia's capital, but Moscow, at once ancient and new-built, was still its first city. In his *History of the Expedition to Russia Undertaken by the Emperor Napoleon in the Year 1812*, French general and historian, Count Philip de Segur, wrote of the Kremlin at the heart of 'Moscow with the golden cupolas', as:

> a lofty triangular fortress; the vast double enclosure of which, half a league in circuit, contained, the one, several palaces, some churches, and rocky and uncultivated spots; the other, a prodigious bazaar, the town of the merchants and shopkeepers, where was displayed the collected wealth of the four quarters of the globe.

NAPOLEON AND NICHOLASES

Nicolas Goss's representation of the fateful 1807 Tilsit meeting of Napoleon, Alexander I and Louise and Friedrich Wilhelm III of Prussia. The Franco-Russian treaty did not last long. (Public domain)

By the 19th century, it seemed accepted that the purpose of the Kremlin was simply as an architectural celebration of Russian wealth and glory. Older buildings were demolished, including the dilapidated Heraldic Tower (see below), to make way for airy open spaces and new construction in brightly coloured, pseudo-Gothic style. The thought of the Kremlin as a fortress seemed a fanciful archaicism. And then came Napoleon. In 1812, his Grande Armée, the largest field force in history, cut its way deep into European Russia, and after it bloodily broke through Marshal Mikhail Kutuzov's forces at Borodino, Moscow was there for the taking.

But not for enjoying. Napoleon had won a city that was all but deserted and emptied of provisions. In the words of General Armand de Caulaincourt:

> In the Kremlin, just like in most private mansions, everything was in place: even the clock went on, as if the owners remained at home. A city without inhabitants was surrounded by gloomy silence. Throughout our long journey we did not meet a single local resident; the army held positions in the vicinity; some corps were placed in barracks. At three o'clock the emperor mounted his horse, travelled around the Kremlin, … visited the two most important bridges and returned to the Kremlin, where he settled in the ceremonial chambers of Emperor Alexander.

Napoleon had assumed that Tsar Alexander I, on losing what was still Russia's largest city, would sue for peace. He was wrong.

Burning Moscow

The French forces billeted themselves wherever they chose: the Emperor himself ensconced himself in the Kremlin. Within a day, however, he was fleeing, as fires engulfed several neighbourhoods of the city. The French claimed that this was arson conducted on the orders of Count Fyodor Rostopchin, former governor of the city: 'Moscow itself was designed to be a great infernal machine, the sudden nocturnal explosion of which was to consume the Emperor and his army,' wrote de Segur. In any case, once again strong winds sent the flames rolling across the largely wooden city, and risked surrounding the Kremlin. De Segur recounted that 'we were encircled by a sea of fire, which blocked up all the gates of the citadel, and frustrated the first attempts that were made to depart'.

Napoleon was evacuated through an underground passage that led to the banks of the Moskva, and took shelter in the Petrovsky Palace to the north-west, safely away from the fires. Once they had subsided, Napoleon returned to the Kremlin, which he made his court, headquarters and bastion. Entertainers sought to divert him, his troops drilled on Cathedral Square, messengers took orders back to Paris, and he constantly toyed with plans for a march on St Petersburg, all the while brooding on why Alexander would not come to terms. Meanwhile, he had the Kremlin's defences shored up, in case the Russians came to retake it by force.

They never did, though. As Marshal Kutuzov and Marshal Prince Joachim-Napoléon Murat fought a duel of manoeuvre across European Russia, autumn marched towards winter, and food for Napoleon's men and fodder for their horses became harder and harder to find. In October, he accepted the inevitable and began the long, bloody retreat that would see his Grande Armée whittled away by hunger, desertion and Cossack raids. Before he left, though, he ordered his Governor-General of Moscow, Marshal Édouard Mortier, to finish the job of destroying city and Kremlin alike, to leave it 'a heap of ruins, a filthy and unwholesome sink, without importance, either political or military'.

The Palace of Facets was put to the torch, and barrels of gunpowder stacked around the Kremlin walls and towers. Slow-matches were set to

Viktor Masurovsky's *The Fire of Moscow* allows itself considerable artistic licence, not least as Napoleon had left before the fires were set, but it conveys the scale of the blaze. (Public domain)

detonate the mines after the last French troops had left. The effort was hurried and half-hearted, however, and some of the gunpowder apparently had become damp. The attempt symbolically to rip the heart out of Moscow was more failure than success. Stretches of the walls were damaged, but only the Vodovzvodnaya Tower was brought down. Three other towers and the Senate were battered. The Ivan the Great Belltower survived intact: one of the officers in the Russian force relieving the city said, on seeing that, 'so long as the bells chime, the Kremlin endures'.

Rebuilt, repurposed

Moscow was three-quarters destroyed, not least as Russians looted what they could after the French withdrew. The Kremlin had survived better, but was again neither defensible nor a fitting royal residence. Restoring the Kremlin was a priority. The architect Fyodor Sokolov was charged with leading the project, and at speed, although it would take 20 years before the last signs of devastation were erased. The walls were quickly rebuilt as they had been, as well as most of the damaged towers. As the Arsenal was being repaired, captured French guns – the 12-pounder Gribeauval cannon, which Napoleon used to call his *belles filles* (beautiful daughters) – were placed outside it.

Later, Tsar Nicholas I would build a new Grand Kremlin Palace, but the rest of the century saw little further change to the Kremlin beyond restoration and the addition of some statuary. With the capital still being in St Petersburg, the Kremlin became something of a civic amenity. Most of it was open to visitors when the tsar was not in residence. In the later part of the century, as unrest and terrorism became a greater challenge to a regime which was looking increasingly antiquated, the garrison and members of the paramilitary Gendarmerie stepped up their searches of visitors by the end of the century. It was a sign of the times – and a harbinger of coming troubles.

The opulence of the Grand Kremlin Palace is evident from this picture of President Putin speaking at a reception for military cadets in its faithfully reconstructed Andreyevsky Hall. (Alexei Druzhinin\TASS via Getty Images)

RED FORTRESS

In 1905, hunger and anger at Russia's defeat at the hands of the Japanese, had created a volatile environment across the country. The spark that ignited it was the 'Bloody Sunday' massacre in St Petersburg, when guards at the tsar's Winter Palace gunned down peaceful protesters. The 1905 Revolution was not a single, coherent struggle, but a collection of local insurrections, by an equally wide range of political movements, and it was their lack of unity that ensured the regime was able to survive, picking off its challengers one by one.

1905: the holdout

This was certainly evident in Moscow, where arguably the Kremlin and the Nikolayevsky Railway Station (now called the Leningrad Station) share the claim to have saved the city for the tsar. An alliance of revolutionary groups called a general strike, and when Vice Admiral Fyodor Dubasov, governor of Moscow, tried to arrest its ringleaders, this precipitated an uprising. The Joint Council of Volunteer Fighting Squads organized a force of more than 2,000 workers and students, and armed them with weapons secretly stockpiled for just such an event or else seized from a police force that was wholly unequal to this threat.

The Moscow garrison fought back, shelling the Joint Council's headquarters and making periodic sallies into working-class neighbourhoods, but their commanders feared that the soldiers, many of whom were locally recruited, would mutiny if pushed too hard. Meanwhile, the headquarters of the Okhrana political police was bombed, and its Moscow chief killed. The industrial Presnensky neighbourhood, west of the Kremlin, with its textile factories and dense workers' housing, became a revolutionary stronghold, its streets barricaded and patrolled by militia. By 12 December, the garrison had essentially been pushed back into the Kremlin and six of the city's seven railway stations had fallen to the revolutionaries.

The situation for the government forces seemed dire, but the Kremlin was still a formidable challenge for revolutionary militias, especially as its defenders had two of the army's rare new imported 1895 Maxim machine guns, which could sweep the wide-open spaces of Red Square or the banks of the Moskva. More importantly, for all the talk of a Joint Council, the revolutionary groups were divided, with most Presnensky militias content just to hold their own neighbourhoods. As a result, the Kremlin was able to

This panorama from an early film shows the Kremlin's Ivanovskaya Square in 1908, showing from left to right the Tsar Bell, Chudov Monastery, the Cathedral of the Annunciation and the Small Nikolayevsky Palace. (Public domain)

Major General Georgi Min, the uncompromising and energetic commander who crushed the 1905 rising in Moscow. (Public domain)

A Fiat-Izhorsky armoured car pressed into Red Guard service. Such assets were to prove battle-winners in the messy, close-quarters urban combat of the 1917 Revolution and subsequent Civil War. (Public Domain)

hold out until 15 December, when the Semyonovsky Lifeguard Regiment of the Imperial Guard arrived from St Petersburg at Nikolayevsky Station. An elite unit, its orders were to do whatever was needed to quell the rising. Its commander, General Georgy Min, sent a battalion to relieve the Kremlin, while personally leading the assault into Presnensky, under cover of an artillery bombardment by the regiment's M1877 87mm light field guns. His orders were ruthlessly unambiguous: 'act without mercy. There will be no arrests.' Two days later, the rising had been crushed.

1917: Bolshevik target

The Bolshevik leader Lenin later noted that while the Moscow rising had failed, it had shown how the revolutionary forces needed to organize and act in the future; success would be won 'by learning from the experience of Moscow'. This proved true in the Bolsheviks' seizure of power in 1917. The Great October Revolution, as they called it (though in Western calendars it took place in November) involved an almost bloodless seizure of St Petersburg from a regime exhausted by World War I and lacking any real support from population and army alike. Moscow, though, would be a tougher fight, and the struggle to control the Kremlin proved critical.

The city was a hotbed of Bolshevik support. On the eve of revolution, the Bolsheviks' Moscow Military Revolutionary Committee (MVRK) began to muster its forces, including army elements loyal to their cause. This included many within the Kremlin garrison, elements of the 56th Zhytomyr Infantry Regiment and the 193rd Infantry Reserve Regiment. They let workers into the complex, where Colonel Nikolai Viskovsky, chief of the Arsenal, allowed 1,500 rifles and ammunition to be distributed to workers' militias.

They controlled the Kremlin, but were hemmed in by armed contingents of *yunkers*, loyalist military cadets. Martial law was declared and the government forces – outnumbered but at that time with momentum and discipline on their side – moved armoured cars and a 76mm Putilov M1900 field gun close to the Kremlin. The 193rd Regiment opted to withdraw, and then the remaining revolutionary forces, cut off from the MVRK and accepting their enemies' over-optimistic claim that they controlled the rest of the city, surrendered.

What happened next is disputed. Two companies of cadets entered the Kremlin to oversee the surrender and, as the revolutionaries began to lay down their guns in Senate Square, firing began. Communist sources later claimed that the cadets staged a massacre, while surviving cadets said it was the revolutionaries who had set a trap, luring them in to be ambushed by emplaced riflemen in the upper stories of the Arsenal. An official report at the time, though, suggests this was bad luck, that jumpy cadets opened fire when they heard shots from elsewhere in the city, thinking they were being shot at. Either way, six cadets and some 200 pro-Bolshevik soldiers were killed or wounded – and the Kremlin was again in government hands.

The situation was precarious, though. The MVRK had serious difficulties controlling its forces given that government troops held the telegraph office and telephone exchange. However, this was not 1905: the Bolsheviks were more disciplined, they understood the importance of concentrating force, they were supported by a number of army officers, and they were ruthless and forceful in ensuring that local units obeyed their orders. They also made sure they controlled all the railway stations this time, but, in any case, there were no government forces available to help relieve Moscow's defenders. It was just a matter of time.

The MVRK was soon able to gather its forces, especially Red Guards from the outer industrial suburbs, and surrounded the Kremlin, shelling it with a collection of artillery pieces, including M1910 122mm howitzers. Battered, isolated, hungry and seemingly abandoned, the Kremlin's defenders surrendered after a day's bombardment, and the city was the Bolsheviks'.

Soviet power

Stretches of the walls and the Spasskaya, Nikolskaya and Beklemishevskaya Towers had all taken damage from shelling (the top of the Beklemishevskaya's spire was sheared off by a shell), but overall the Kremlin was in surprisingly good shape, which helped clinch the decision of the new Bolshevik leadership to move their capital back to Moscow in 1918. The red flag flew over the Kremlin. (Although it would take until 1935 for the double-headed tsarist eagles atop some of the towers to be taken down and ultimately replaced with internally lit ruby stars, as originally placed on the Vodovzvodnaya Tower.)

A plaque on the Kremlin wall commemorating the 70th anniversary of the formation of the Kremlin Guard, now known as the Presidential Regiment. (Author's collection)

From the first, the Bolshevik leadership was under threat and so the Kremlin was again made a fortress. Its garrison was made up of fervent Bolshevik sympathizers. This included Red Guard – soon to become the Red Army – units such as the Latvian Rifles (see box) and soldiers from the Red Army's 1st Moscow Machine Gun Training Courses. Security troops of the newly formed political police, the All-Russian Emergency Commission for Combating Counter-Revolution and Sabotage (VChK, but generally known as the Cheka) were also stationed there. In 1935, Kremlin security became solely the responsibility of the Special Purpose Battalion (BosNaz). In 1936, the Directorate of the Moscow Kremlin

Commandant (UKMK) was formally transferred from military to Department 1 of the political police, by that time called the People's Commissariat for Internal Affairs (NKVD). That year, the Kremlin Guard was expanded to regimental strength. In 1952, it would be renamed the Independent Special Forces Regiment (OPSpN) and in 1973 the Independent Red Banner Kremlin KGB Regiment.

The Latvian Rifles

In 1915, the Russian government drafted a Latvian Rifle Division from its occupied Baltic territories, to contribute to the war effort. They fought well, and the force was eventually expanded to a total of eight line regiments and one reserve, organized in two brigades. Resentment grew in the ranks as they felt they were being used as cannon-fodder by the Russians. In the Revolution, significant numbers joined the Red Guard, most being formed into Red Latvian Rifle units under Colonel Jukums Vācietis (who would, for ten months, be first commander-in-chief of the newly formed Workers' and Peasants' Red Army). They distinguished themselves fighting against the 'White' counter-revolutionary forces, and such was their loyalty and efficiency that they also became the Bolshevik leadership's Praetorian Guard. A company of 328 Latvian Riflemen accompanied Lenin to Moscow and they became part of the Kremlin garrison.

Red Square in 1929, showing the newly built Lenin Mausoleum, in front of the Senate Tower. (ETH-Bibliothek Zürich, Bildarchiv / Fotograf: Heim, Arnold/Dia_023-029/ CC BY-SA 4.0)

The Soviets stamped their mark on the Kremlin. Whitewashed walls again became red. Statues to tsars and dukes were toppled, icons removed, and imperial symbols chiselled off walls. In the 1930s, the last remnants of the Kitay-Gorod walls were demolished. Gold was stripped from church domes and sumptuous interiors, in some cases as a prelude to destruction. At the start of 1917, there were 31 churches within the Kremlin walls: by 1941 only 14 were left, and most were either closed or repurposed. The Chudov Monastery, for example, became the Kremlin hospital, before being bulldozed to make way for new construction. The Cathedral of the Saviour on Bor, the oldest church in Moscow, was replaced with office buildings. Overall, of the 54 individual buildings that comprised the complex at the start of the Soviet era, only 26 survived to its end in 1991.

Instead, offices and new security posts proliferated. The Grand Kremlin Palace

---

E WWII

Facing the very real threat of German bombing, a major effort was launched to camouflage the Kremlin by a variety of means. Here, Red Square has been repainted to give an impression of streets, roofs and courtyards, while the Lenin Mausoleum has been hidden from view under a fake wood-and-canvas building. The Spasskaya Tower has been camouflaged in shades of grey and green and its clocks covered, while the Senate Tower has simply been repainted. A mock-up apartment building frontage, like a theatrical backdrop, has been added to part of the wall, and more fake buildings, generally just wood shells, erected inside the Kremlin, between the Senate and Spasskaya Towers. Of course, the protections were also more active: barrage balloons are visible to the left and two Polikarpov I-153 biplane fighters fly overhead.

became a meeting hall for the Soviets, and the Palace of Facets, a cafeteria. In the early years of Soviet power, when security was still an issue, most of the leadership not only worked but lived within the Kremlin's walls: 2,100 people were officially resident as of 1920, in the middle of the Civil War. By the 1930s, this number diminished sharply both as the security situation improved and new, spacious housing for the Communist Party elite was built. By 1939, only 31 people were still registered there, including Stalin (though he actually spent much of his time at his country residence at Kuntsevo).

Great Patriotic War

In 1941, when Nazi Germany invaded, the Kremlin was once again under threat, both from air attack and from the determined drive to take Moscow: at the start of the war, Adolf Hitler reportedly personally ordered that a special unit of sappers be formed comprehensively to demolish the Kremlin when it was captured.

The capital was ringed with the anti-air-defences of the Special Moscow Air Defence Army. As well as 17 fighter aircraft regiments, this included 15 AA artillery divisions, four searchlight divisions, three AA MG divisions, three barrage balloon divisions, and numerous other units. It had guns ranging from 37mm M1939 61-Ks and 25mm M1940 72-K light cannon, to large 85mm M1939 52-Ks emplaced throughout the city, especially on elevations such as the Lenin and Poklonnaya Hills. Barrage balloons sprouted in parks and squares. Quad-mounted 7.62mm PM M1910 HMGs were emplaced on the roof of the Grand Kremlin Palace, the Armoury and other buildings, supplemented by a battery of M1939 guns.

However, the Soviets also relied on *maskirovka*, deception. The Kremlin was artfully camouflaged to look like just another city neighbourhood. The red stars which had previously burned brightly atop the towers were removed and plywood structures built over some of the spires to obscure their distinctive silhouettes. The green roofs of the main buildings were repainted rust-red and brown to look like regular tiles, the church domes grey. The thick walls were painted to look from above like streets or rows of buildings, complete with fake doors and windows. Across the Alexandrovsky Gardens, a canvas 'street' was laid to the nearby embankment, again to make this look

The Kremlin was not the only national treasure treated to *maskirovka* – camouflage and deception – in World War II. Here the Bolshoi Theatre has been painted to look like houses and break up its distinctive shape. (RIA Novosti archive, image #42402 / Alexander Krasavin / CC-BY-SA 3.0)

like a residential neighbourhood. The distinctive mausoleum built to house Lenin's preserved remains after his death in 1924 was masked by a wood-and-canvas fake two-storey building. The broad cobbled expanse of Red Square, a potential navigation point for German bombers, was painted with roofs and later filled with mock buildings.

Between the city's dense air-defences and the camouflage, the Kremlin was kept safe. Although it was deemed a particular target, it was bombed only eight times: five times in 1941 and three in 1942. Fifteen high-explosive bombs, 151 incendiaries and

An air raid over Moscow, with the Kremlin silhouetted by German flare. (Margaret Bourke-White/The LIFE Picture Collection via Getty Images)

several flares were dropped on the Kremlin and its immediate surroundings. In total, 94 people were killed, the largest single casualties coming in August 1941, when a 1000kg bomb hit the Arsenal right next to an anti-air machine-gun station, and in October, when a 500kg bomb hit the courtyard outside the Arsenal just as people were streaming to bomb shelters, killing 41.

Overall, though, the Kremlin survived virtually intact. Only the Alarm and Spasskaya Towers suffered any real damage. In part, this was thanks to the work of the Kremlin's own military fire brigade detachment and also the Kremlin Guard. As well as policing strict new security measures – including the compulsory disarmament of any visitors to the Kremlin, even senior army officers – more than 100 were at any time assigned to extinguishing any incendiaries which might fall, and around two dozen mounted a round-the-clock watch from the roof of the Grand Kremlin Palace.

Of course, no one knew that this would work, and so in the 1930s a command bunker had been dug in the Izmailovo neighbourhood to the north-east, the Reserve Command Post of the Supreme Commander-in-Chief. This luxuriously appointed vault – with wood-panelled quarters, a large conference room and even an auditorium – was connected to the Kremlin by a 17km-long underground tunnel, down which Stalin and his lieutenants would be sped in ZIS-101 limousines in time of crisis from the mouth, right under the Spasskaya Tower. Like much of the Moscow metro system, the tunnel was largely dug by Gulag convicts, many of whom were then transferred to the higher-mortality labour camps in the far north and east to prevent their being able to reveal the project. The bunker, under the Izmailovo Stadium, is now a museum. There are also accounts of a tunnel between the Defence Ministry buildings at 37 Myasnitskaya Street and the Kremlin. However, as this is essentially on the way to Izmailovo, it is more likely that this was simply a spur onto the main route. The tunnel was allowed to fall into disrepair with the construction of the secret 'Metro-2' lines after the war (see below), although the stretch closer to the Kremlin was blocked to prevent it being used to bypass the security perimeter.

The Kremlin in the nuclear age

Victory in 1945 left the USSR acknowledged as one of the two world superpowers and the last major construction project in the Kremlin reflected its new-found status: a massive and pompous Palace of Congresses, which

The Middle Arsenal Tower incorporates a faux grotto in its base, commemorating victory over Napoleon, made of rubble from buildings destroyed during the French occupation of Moscow. The obelisk, erected in 1814, celebrates the Romanov tsars. (Author's collection)

required the demolition of yet more older buildings. (Nonetheless, in 1990 the Kremlin was added to the UNESCO World Heritage List.) Security for the Kremlin remained the responsibility of the same people, but with a reorganization of the security forces in 1954, the Guards Directorate of the Ministry of State Security (MGB) became the Ninth Directorate of the new Committee of State Security (KGB).

The Kremlin Guard was awarded the Order of the Red Banner in 1965 for its exploits during the Great Patriotic War, becoming the Independent Red Banner Special Purpose KGB Regiment under the USSR Council of Ministers. In 1973, it was again renamed, as the Independent Red Banner Kremlin KGB Regiment. This was an elite unit, and recruits (both volunteers and conscripts) had to have impeccable Party references, no criminal record, and look the part which, in practice, usually meant tall and Slavic. Some wore militia (police) uniforms for duties in Red Square and the Alexandrovsky Gardens, but most wore regular KGB military uniforms, essentially patterned after the army's, but with dark-blue collar tabs, epaulettes, cap bands and arm of service badges on their left sleeves. Their epaulettes were marked GB, for State Security. While the SKS carbine was retained for ceremonial use, such as the minutely choreographed changing of the guard outside Lenin's Memorial – so-called Guard Post Number One – the Kremlin Guard were early adopters of the AK-47 assault rifle and later the AK-74. The standard sidearm was the PM Makarov, while SVD sniper's rifles, machine guns and man-portable anti-tank and anti-air systems were stored out of sight for emergencies.

However, this was also the nuclear age, to which the defences of the Kremlin offered no protection. Part of the answer was to build downwards, to dig bunkers and a network of escape routes. A huge mythology has emerged about the so-called 'Metro-2' secret government transport system under Moscow, and Ramenki, where the Soviets, in the 1960s and 1970s, were thought to have built a massive underground city able to house up to 15,000 people, with food supplies to last 30 years. The truth is less dramatic than the stories, but nonetheless demonstrates that the Kremlin became the hub of an extensive subterranean network.

Most details about Metro-2 are still classified, although there have been sufficient leaks and official statements to be able to confirm its overall outline, especially as members of the intrepid Diggers of the Underground Planet urban exploration group came across an entrance to it when exploring the recesses of the civilian metro network in 1994. It was begun in Stalin's times, although only commissioned in 1967. The first line was an evacuation route, running south-west from the Kremlin to the government airport of Vnukovo-2, via a stop at Ramenki near the Moscow State University campus, then a KGB (now Federal Security Service – FSB) facility and the General Staff Academy. At Ramenki, according to former Moscow mayor Gavriil Popov, there is no fabled underground city (that would in any case likely have created serious subsidence issues in the city above), but a depot and a maintenance station.

Later, at least two other lines were built. One, completed in 1987, was codenamed D-6 and is supposed to run from the Kremlin all the way to a command bunker at Voronovo, 56km south of Moscow. The third, finished at the same time, is rather shorter, stretching from the Kremlin, via the old headquarters of the KGB on Lubyanka Square (now also one of the FSB's HQs) to the deep command bunker of the Moscow air defence network at 33 Myasnitskaya Street. It was then extended to the newer, more extensive air defence command centre at Zarya, east of Moscow.

The regular Moscow metro, an undoubted triumph of mass transit, is relatively deep (in part for geological reasons, in part because the stations and tunnels were also envisaged as potential bomb shelters), generally running 35–55m underground. The D-6 line is even deeper, 50–210m under the streets. The spartan Metro-2 tunnels have no live rail because the system uses short L-type battery-electric or, in some cases, DPS-01 diesel-electric trains. The tracks are recessed into reinforced concrete slabs so that, if necessary, compact RAF-977 minibuses (and later RAF-2203s) could be used in the tunnels.

These secret lines appear to have fallen into disuse in the 1990s, because of the end of the Cold War and budgetary pressures. That Vladimir Putin also favours travel to and from the Kremlin by helicopter may also be a factor. Nevertheless, surveillance cameras were fitted on platforms and entry points in the 1980s, and more modern access control systems in the 2000s. The system is under the control of the Main Directorate of Special Programs of the President of the Russian Federation (GUSP PRF), a federal agency within the Presidential Administration with a strikingly broad and mysterious remit. Its Special Facilities Service – which also looks after presidential residences – includes Military Unit 52581, which provides security and support specifically for the Kremlin.

A US KH-7 spy satellite photo of the 'Dog House' radar at Kubinka from 1967, part of the system built to defend the Kremlin from nuclear attack. (Public domain)

Moscow ABM defences

Hardened bunkers and underground escape tunnels are all very well, but the Soviet leaderships also wanted to protect themselves from potential nuclear attack in a more active way. In 1956, work began on a prototype anti-ballistic missile system. The A-35 system became active in 1971, comprising two Dunay-3 radar stations at Kubinka east of Moscow (with the NATO codenames Dog House and Cat House, respectively) and Chekhov to the south, and four launch sites with 16 A-350 missiles (NATO designation ABM-1 Galosh) and three tracking and homing radars. Even so, all together the expectation was that the whole system could at best protect Moscow and the Kremlin from a single ICBM or up to six intermediate-range missiles. In 1995, the A-135 system replaced this, with the Don-2N battle management phased array radar at Sofrino refining data from the country's wider early-warning network, and five launch sites with a total of 68 53T6 (ABM-3 Gazelle) short-range interceptor missiles. Until 2003, it also included two sites with silos for 16 51T6 (ABM-4 Gorgon) longer-range exoatmospheric missiles, but these were then decommissioned as no longer usable. While an improvement on A-35, the assumption is still that this could only stop two advanced ICBMs or up to 35 intermediate-range missiles. A follow-on system, provisionally named A-235, is still under development.

TWENTY TOWERS

The 20 towers around the Kremlin walls (and one now-defunct one within the complex, the Heraldic) all share a common architectural style, apart from the Nikolskaya Tower, rebuilt at the beginning of the 19th century as pseudo-Gothic. With the exception of the Tsar's Tower, all were constructed in the late 15th century as red-brick, flat-topped structures (often on the site of a previous tower), with *varnitsy* – loopholes with hinged wooden covers – as well as larger machicolations and firing positions. Originally topped with pyramidal or conical wooden roofs, the following century they acquired the distinctive tall turrets, brick-built and sheathed in green-glazed tiles, visible today. The following list gives the date of first construction of each tower.

First and Second Nameless (1480s)
The First and Second Nameless Towers are plain bastions along the Moskva, between the Tainitskaya and Petrovskaya Towers, whose peculiar appellation, Bezymyannaya, apparently stems from the tradition of naming towers after nearby aristocratic estates. These were close to the commoners' *posad*, which offered no such options. The First is also sometimes called the Powder Tower, because of the gunpowder magazines inside it – which led to its first destruction in 1571 during the Great Fire of Moscow. For a while, a smithy was located in the base of the Second and there was a postern gate through the walls, although it is unclear when this was sealed. In the early 18th century, a double earthen rampart, faced with oak logs, was built in front of the towers, but later removed. The First is 34m tall and the Second just 30m, and the last time they saw any kind of action was in 1917, when they were shelled by the Red Guard.

Alarm (1495)
The Nabatnaya or Alarm Tower acquired its name after the construction of the Tsar's Tower in 1680 led to it acquiring the bell from an old wooden lookout. Thereafter, it was used to warn against fires and similar hazards, until the bell was removed in 1817. It had been forged specially to sound differently from the church bells that were so common in Moscow and the Kremlin, so that people would know when there was an alarm. Originally simply a defensive structure, it was built as a heavy-set square-based fortress with no external gate, and walls 2.5m thick at the base, penetrated by deep loopholes, and with caponiers, firing trenches adjacent to the walls half-covered with wooden slats. Its spire brought its height to 38m. There was an observation post high in the spire, and passages through the main wall connected it to the Konstantino-Yeleninskaya and Spasskaya Towers, later used to store cannonballs and gunpowder. An underground tunnel led out away from the walls, as an escape or sally route. In the 1970s, subsidence led to cracking in the foundations of the tower. Although it was stabilized, it still stands slightly out of true.

Annunciation (1487–88)
This 31m tower was a major strongpoint along the river wall, deliberately built to extend beyond it, so first archers and then musketeers could fire along the walls at those seeking to scale it. A broad upper tier hung over the lower levels of the tower, with machicolations from which tar or boiling

water could be poured down onto attackers. The tower was used as a prison during the reign of Ivan the Terrible, and acquired a grim reputation for the tortures visited on the tsar's enemies. The story is that in response to the prayers of one benighted prisoner, the icon of the Annunciation of the Most Holy Theotokos (the Virgin Mary) miraculously appeared on the inner wall, and so it was renamed *Blagoveschenskaya* (Annunciation) after this miracle, although cynics might suggest that its reputation had become so bloody that Ivan's successors simply wanted to signal a break with the past. In the 17th century, a postern gate was opened towards the river. It was used by Kremlin laundrywomen, and also to unload food supplies brought by raft along the river, to be stored in the adjacent Zhitny Dvor, the Grain Yard. This gate was closed when Peter the Great ordered a reinforcement of the Kremlin. The tower's loopholes were widened for larger guns, and a *bolverk* outwork was built in front of it, a wood-fronted earthen bastion that survived into the early 19th century.

This 1910 map of the Kremlin superimposes the layout of the day with demolished buildings and former defences, including the old outer ramparts along what had been the Neglinnaya River and towards Red Square. (Public domain)

Armoury (1493–95)

The 39m-tall Armoury Tower was originally the Konyushennaya or Stables Tower, after the nearby government buildings, but was renamed in 1851, when they were replaced by the Armoury. Sitting as it did then on the banks of the Neglinnaya River, considerable work had to be made shoring up its foundations, and after it was built the territory beyond it remained an unsightly and swampy stretch of ponds and water-logged ditches, which were left to hinder any attacker. Originally a two-storey brick building with no access outside the walls, nor even loopholes on the lower storey, in the early 1600s it acquired a brick parapet with merlons, then in 1676 to 1686 a stone upper level with a watchtower, as well as a postern gate to allow access to the stables (bricked up again at the beginning of the 18th century). By the 19th century, with the creation of the Alexandrovsky Gardens just outside the walls, the tower had no military role or, indeed, any other purpose; it remains essentially empty to this day.

Beklemishevskaya (1488)

Named after the nearby estate of the Beklemishevs, this cylindrical tower anchors the south-eastern corner of the Kremlin by the Bolshoy (Large) Moskvoretsky Bridge and is thus also known as the Moskvoretskaya Tower. This is a natural defensive location – it was also a corner of Dmitry Donskoi's Kremlin, and its round shape allows defenders to cover the southern wall, the approaches to the eastern wall and the Spassky Gates, and also the ford

over the Moskva which predated the bridge. It was connected to the *Bely Gorod* walls until their removal. Atop its three vaulted floors, a battlement was later built, bringing the tower up to its 46m height. The internal staircases between floors are steep and narrow, to make it harder for any attacker seeking to fight their way up the tower. There was reportedly a secret underground passage leading to the banks of the Moskva, although this is still disputed. Given its strength and also the presence of a full-time garrison, the tower was also a place to store high-status prisoners. The bodies of prisoners who had succumbed to torture would simply be thrown out of the tower, into a ditch along the river. The Beklemishevskaya is unique as the only Kremlin tower not to have ever been destroyed, dismantled, or required major renovations. It even survived the 1917 Revolution relatively unscathed, though loyalist troops emplaced machine guns in the tower to cover the Bolshoy Moskvoretsky Bridge.

In 2015, the Beklemishevskaya Tower was in the news when opposition figure Boris Nemtsov was assassinated while walking across the bridge, and controversy erupted over whether or not the numerous security cameras on the tower had captured footage of the murder. This picture of the impromptu shrine to Nemtsov shows the proximity of the tower. (Author's collection)

Borovitskaya (1490)

This 54m gate tower stands on what is likely to be the spot where the very first stockade was built, at the crest of the hill of the same name. Certainly, this is where Dmitry Donskoi built his *detinets*. Originally known as the Forerunner Tower after the nearby church of St John the Baptist, this connected the Kremlin to the *podol* mercantile quarter outside. Everything from mead breweries to cookhouses occupied a sprawling collection of stalls and lean-tos on both sides of the wall, between the Trinity and Borovitsky Gates. As such, it was for most of its existence a working rather than ceremonial gate. Its lower status meant that it was sometimes used precisely to avoid attention – chroniclers recorded that Grand Duke Vasily III (r. 1505–33), eager to return to his palace when he was sick, and wanting to keep this from foreign ambassadors staying in the Kremlin, once stole in through the Borovitsky Gates precisely for this reason.

Underground passages led to concealed exits on the other side of the moat. Most were later collapsed or filled in, but to this day there remains no comprehensive survey of these hidden routes. In the 17th century, a tall turret brought the Borovitskaya to its current eight storeys, and its fine decorations concealed a range of loopholes and machicolations. A guardhouse was built on the other side of the moat, and the fixed bridge replaced by a drawbridge controlled from within the tower. Later, an earthwork *bolverk* was also built to shield the entry to the tower in the middle of what is now Borovitskaya Square.

In the Soviet era, this gate was often used by official motorcades, and in 1969, a disgruntled army officer made an unsuccessful assassination attempt on Communist Party General Secretary Leonid Brezhnev as he was being driven towards the gate. Today it is again largely reserved for the entry and exit of presidential motorcades. As such, the adjacent Borovitskaya Square is under constant supervision by the traffic police (and Kremlin Guard in traffic police uniforms), able to control all the traffic lights for blocks around to ensure an empty road when the president is on the move.

Commandant's (1495)

A middle-height (41m) tower, it was originally called the Kolymazhnaya Tower after a nearby estate, which housed the prince's carriages and sleighs. Then known as the Deaf Tower, it was finally renamed when the Moscow Commandant moved his residence to the adjacent Amusements Palace in 1806. This stretch of land along the original route of the Neglinnaya River was prone to flooding and so when he planned the tower, Aleviz Fryazin – who specialized in such works and would later build a dam on the river – put considerable effort into shoring up the bank with arches. Even so, the tower suffered from water seeping into its foundations, so in the 17th century it was reinforced with a talus of rock fragments at its base and buttresses. The tower was built to be an independent bastion, with no gates on the outside (which is why it was called Deaf) but many loopholes and fighting platforms. One of the earthen *bolverk*s built in 1707, the Neglinny, was directly in front of the tower, although later it would fall into disrepair; attempts to restore it at the end of the century only managed to create a swamp at the base of the tower, later drained.

The *Poteshny Dvorets*, or Palace of Amusements, is the last surviving example of a boyar estate within the Kremlin. Built in 1651 for Ilya Miloslavsky, its onion-domed towers belie the essential solidity of the building: this was constructed to be defensible. For a while it became a place for the tsars' families to relax, hence its name, but it is now the offices of the Kremlin Commandant and his staff. (www.kremlin.ru/ CC 4.0)

Corner Arsenal (1492)

The most massive of the towers, this 60m-tall fortification anchored not just the northern edge of the Kremlin's walls, but later connected to those of Kitay-Gorod. It commanded the crossing of the Neglinnaya River to the Great Market on the far bank. A faceted drum with 16 faces, an octagonal spire, and walls fully 4m thick at the base, its shape allowed its defenders to fire in every direction, so its eight tiers of loopholes went all the way round, also facing into the Kremlin. It had its own well and deep storage vaults, as well as a passage through the curtain wall to the Nikolskaya Tower. Inside, the upper floors could only be reached by ladders which the defenders could pull up to hinder any attackers.

In 1707, the Resurrection *bolverk* was built in front of it, although this earthwork fell into disrepair after the end of the Great Northern War. The tower was damaged when the Arsenal was blown up by the retreating French in 1812. In the late 19th century, it was briefly used as an archive, but now it is once again wholly a part of the Kremlin defences, housing a unit of the Presidential Regiment.

Heraldic (1636, demolished 1801)

Because the Kolymazhny Gate was inside the Kremlin walls when the red-brick perimeter was built, it did not acquire a gate tower until a century and a half later, largely for ceremonial reasons, as a way into the compound of the royal palace. A square-based four-storey tower, it acquired its name from the coats of arms of various Imperial possessions and cities around its faces. Built in classic style, nonetheless, it fell into disrepair in the 18th century and with no clear purpose, was demolished in 1801, the Grand Kremlin Palace later being built over its site.

Konstantino-Yeleninskaya (1490)

Built on the site of the old Timofeyevsky Gate, the 37m SS. Constantine and Helen Tower was once the main gateway into the complex, its broad archway suited to military sallies and commercial traffic alike. Outside the gates was the Great Posad mercantile quarter, and the Vsekhsvyatskaya (later Varvarka) road, along which rich merchants and nobles built their estates. The other end of the bridge over the Kremlin moat was originally protected by a wooden guardhouse, but in the early 16th century, this was rebuilt in stone. This also became used as a prison from the late 17th century and was thus manned by up to 30 *Streltsy* – and after their rebellion against Peter the Great, a number of their own leaders ended up here, now watched by regular soldiers. As usual, legends arose, including that a never-drying bloody stain marked the walls of the prison. After all, it had become known as *Pitoshny*, 'Torturous', for the terrible fate awaiting its inmates. When the guardhouse was demolished in the 18th century, the tale effortlessly transferred to the Konstantino-Yeleninskaya tower itself. These days, the Kremlin helipad is on the Secret Garden behind the walls, between this and the Beklemishevskaya Tower, so Federal Protection Service (FSO) spotters and snipers regularly take up positions on its top when the president is arriving or leaving by air.

Kutafiya (1516)

This relatively low tower – it is only 13.5m tall – is the last surviving *otvodnaya strelnitsa*, securing the far end of a bridge. The horseshoe-shaped bastion was built by Aleviz Fryazin to guard the access to the Trinity Gate, with a tower added atop the openwork upper tier in the 17th century. It had three gates: one on each side allowed access into the tower across ditches crossed by drawbridges, and the third led across the Neglinnaya River to the Trinity Tower, into the Kremlin itself. This was originally by a low wooden bridge with a central drawbridge, but, in 1516, it was replaced by a stone bridge. Later, the level of the river was raised by dams, such that the ditches became moats, and the tower sat on its own island. Attackers would have to take a snaking embankment path to the drawbridges, slowing them down and ensuring they spent as long as possible under the defenders' fire.

At the turn of the 17th century, when the *Bely Gorod* walls were built, so too was a new stone wall around the Trinity Tower, and the Kutafiya Tower became less of a bastion and more of a ceremonial station for religious and royal processions. The moats were filled in, and the drawbridges dismantled. By 1665, the tower's garrison had dwindled from 20 soldiers in peacetime and up to 100 in war, to just four men. Napoleon's men first entered the Kremlin through the Kutafiya Tower, and the last of them left this way, too. In the 19th century, it again became a guardhouse, and now it is the entry for visitors to the Kremlin, with a controversial glass pavilion added to the side to house ticket offices.

Sometimes the old ways are the best. The Federal Protection Service uses 12 goshawks, eagle owls and peregrine falcons to scare crows and pigeons away from the Kremlin, but now they are also being trialled as answers to smaller drones. They roost in the turret of the Konstantino-Yeleninskaya Tower. (Alexander Nemenov/AFP via Getty Images)

Middle Arsenal (1493–95)

Much less imposing than the neighbouring Trinity and Corner Arsenal Towers, this was built on what had been a corner of Donskoi's earlier, smaller Kremlin. A rectangular-based tower topped with a wooden observation turret and pyramidal wooden roof, this building had an essentially plain frontage, with no external gate and just rows of loopholes, and two flat vertical niches on the outside, from which it got its earlier name, the Faceted Tower. It was renamed in the 18th century, with the construction of the new Arsenal, when its brick turret raised it to a height of 39m.

Nikolskaya (1491)

Uniquely rebuilt in 1816–19 in Gothic style, the St Nicholas Tower was originally a gateway fortress, with the usual *otvodnaya strelnitsa* and a wooden drawbridge between them. In the lower levels of the tower, double walls were added to provide additional defence in case of a breach. Passages through the main fortress wall connected this to the Corner Arsenal Tower. An outer ditch, faced with stone, ran from this tower to the Spasskaya Tower, later flooded to form a moat. In the 16th and 17th centuries, Ivanovskaya Square inside the Kremlin was used as a parade and mustering ground, so detachments would march from there, out through this gate. Conversely, when Pozharsky and Minin's Second Militia retook the Kremlin, they entered this way. The tower was therefore also used for military offices and storerooms, with gunpowder and cannonballs kept in underground vaults. As a result, this was also one of the most heavily guarded towers along the wall. In 1707, new redoubts were built in front of the tower, of stone-faced earthworks. Such was the significance of this gate, even while most of the other additional fortifications built at this time were dismantled or allowed to decay, these were maintained until the early 19th century.

Gutted by fire in 1737, the tower was rebuilt in baroque style, with a domed roof. In 1780, it was in sufficient disrepair that it needed another reconstruction, this time acquiring a tall cylindrical brick turret with a conical roof. In 1805–06, the turret was remodelled as a Gothic, octagonal stone spire. In 1917, it was used as a firing position against the Red Guard and was thus damaged by artillery fire from guns placed at the junction of nearby Nikolskaya Street and Bogoyavlensky Lane.

Petrovskaya (1480s)

Originally known as the Third Nameless Tower, this relatively small construction (just 27m tall) was built on the foundations of a tower of

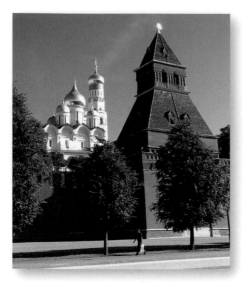

The blocky Tainitskaya Tower was the first of the new brick-built turrets along the Kremlin walls, originally a gateway onto the outer defensive perimeter. (Author's collection)

Dmitry Donskoi's white-stone Kremlin that had been burned down by Tokhtamysh's army. Later, during the 1612 Polish intervention, it was destroyed by artillery fire from across the river, and it was also damaged by French demolition charges in 1812.

Secret (1485)

The reason why an all-too-obvious tower more than 38m tall is called the Tainitskaya or Secret is not because it is inconspicuous, but rather from the hidden well and passage to the Moskva that architect Antonio Gilardi ('Anton Fryazin') included when he built it to replace the Cheshkovy Gates of the former white-stone fortress. It was the first of the new brick-built 15th-century towers, a square-based construct connected by a short bridge to an *otvodnaya strelnitsa* connected to the outer walls along the Moskva, which was only demolished in 1933, in connection with the construction of the embankment. It played a crucial role in the defence of the Kremlin in the 1571 raid by Crimean Khan Devlet-Girey, during which it was badly damaged. It was also used as a fire-watch post, looking out over the Zamoskvorechiye district. Sentries in a small wooden tower on the east side of the gate would ring a bell in alarm when they saw fire over the river. The Secret Tower was dismantled under Catherine II, then rebuilt. In 1863, a wooden platform was added to house cannon and, until 1917, a gun was fired from here to signal noon every day. The gate was sealed in the 1930s.

Senate (1491)

Unlike many of the other towers, the 34m Senate Tower does not appear to have been raised over a previous fortification. Looking out over what is now Red Square, it was purely a defensive structure, relatively austere in looks and with three 'fighting floors' over the ground level, and a flat roof surrounded by crenelations later given a spire. At the base of the Senate Tower, outside the walls, the Soviets established a necropolis. As well as Lenin's Mausoleum, completed in 1930, there is a memorial garden with the ashes of revolutionary heroes from Felix Dzerzhinsky, founder of the Bolshevik political police, to Joseph Stalin. Indeed, the tower narrowly avoided having its top lopped off to mount a statue of Stalin, before he fell from favour. In 1948, a tunnel from the Senate Tower was built to allow Soviet dignitaries to reach the Lenin Mausoleum.

F TRINITY AND KUTAFIYA TOWERS, 1707

Although Peter I – Peter the Great – had largely neglected Moscow and its Kremlin, invasion-scares during the Great Northern War led to reconstruction and expansion of its defences. *Bolverks*, outworks, were built in front of the main towers and gateways, of wooden walls atop berms, with a shallow redan-style v-design around the bridge. Two-gun platforms mount (inset 1) 4-pounder cannon from the Kamensk Iron Foundry. To this end, the old moat along this wall has been cleared of the trees that had grown there since it had been drained. The Trinity Tower is connected to its *otvodnaya*

strelnitsa, the Kutafiya Tower, by a solid bridge, the drawbridge having been removed the century before. Although the Kutafiya Tower had largely lost its defensive role by this stage, acquiring a decorative superstructure of pillars and open 'windows', its roof was still adapted to mounting light 2-pounder guns (inset 2). Since 1680, the walls and towers had been whitewashed to symbolize purity, but the basement of the Trinity Tower still held two 'stone bags', small, unlit cells with no way in or out except through a passage in their floor (inset 3).

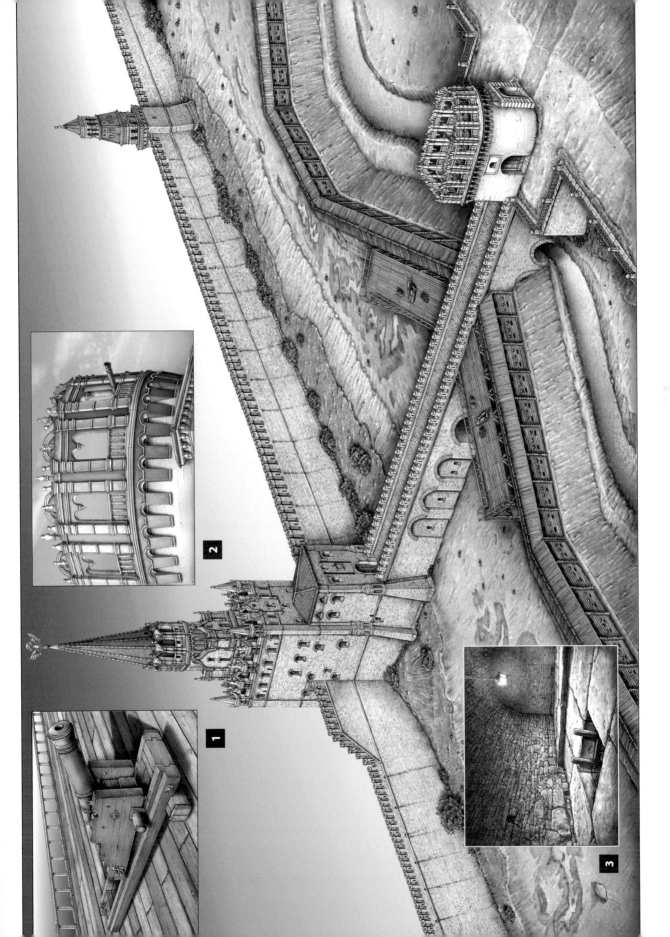

The imposing 67m height of the Spasskaya Tower, one of the main entries to the Kremlin. The gateway was originally considered a holy site: it was regarded as impolite to ride through the gates on horseback, and men were expected to remove their hats. The legend was that when Napoleon – whom the Russians castigated as the Antichrist – rode into the Kremlin through the gate, a strong gust of wind tore the cocked hat from his head. (Author's collection)

Spasskaya (1491)

The Saviour's Tower is perhaps the most recognizable of the Kremlin's gates, leading as it does onto Red Square, and standing 67m tall, plus the illuminated ruby star on its spire. Originally known as the Frolov Tower, after the nearby Church of SS Frol and Lavr, it acquired its present name in 1658. This was the route triumphant tsars and generals would take when returning from campaign and through which would be carried icons being brought to Kremlin churches. In Soviet times, the soldiers goose-stepping their way to Lenin's Mausoleum in Red Square to change the guard, would come from the Spassky Gate, and its chimes signal the start of Victory Day parades and ring in the New Year across the country.

In the construction of the red-brick Kremlin, the tower gained a bridge to an *otvodnaya strelnitsa*, flanked by broad platforms suitable for guards or guns alike, built by Pietro Solari. A portcullis was added to the archway through the Spasskaya Tower itself, and the usual array of loopholes, murder-holes and machicolations on both the tower and its bastion, as well as a tunnel through the wall to the adjacent Alarm Tower. Up to 300 *Streltsy* would rotate through the duties as the so-called 'Arrival Guard' contingent based in an estate just inside the gate – in effect, the emergency response detail. Given that this was the main entry and access point to the Kremlin, particular effort was put into combining elegance with defensibility, the iron-clad oaken gates being decorated with fine gold scrollwork. A hipped wooden turret on the tower's roof mounted a clock and bells, later replaced with a brick tower and rather more elaborate clock. When the Aleviz Ditch was built in 1508 and the Kremlin acquired a moat, a wooden drawbridge connected the tower and its guardhouse. Given the amount of traffic, however, this was soon replaced with an arched stone bridge.

As part of the general fortification work ordered by Peter I, a redan was built in front of the bastion. This V-shaped earthwork was faced with logs, while the scarp or inside bank of the moat was faced with stone to make it harder to scale. In the 19th century, however, these additional fortifications, as well as the bridge, were dismantled as the moat was filled in. The guardhouse did remain, though, until the 20th century. Napoleon's engineers mined the tower, and blockaded the gate with logs and debris, but the fuses did not take and the Russians were able to make the charges safe. On the other hand, the tower was damaged by Bolshevik artillery fire in 1917 and was also slightly damaged by German bombing in 1942.

Trinity (1495)

At 80m, the tallest of the Kremlin towers, the Troitskaya or Trinity Tower is a rectangular-based gate and clock tower connected to the Kutafiya Tower by the Trinity Bridge, and as such is today used by tourists to enter the complex. There has been a tower here since the days of Ivan Kalita, although until 1600 it was just a defensive structure, not a gatehouse. Once rebuilt in brick, it acquired the classic defensive features of the age, with murder-holes in the roof and sides of the 6m-tall archway through the tower, covered *mashikul* loopholes in the lower walls and a covered walkway behind the Kremlin walls to the Middle and Corner Arsenal Towers. As well as the Kutafiya Tower, it was originally also protected by another outwork redoubt to the right of the gate, although this was later dismantled.

Originally, it also had a two-level basement, which included an underground passage into the Kremlin Garden and cells for prisoners, who were executed at the Trinity Gates. By the end of the 17th century, these had fallen into disuse and disrepair. At that time, the tower was still known by a variety of names including the Epiphany and Kuretnaya (after the gates of the same name of the royal palace) Tower, but in 1658 it was officially dubbed Trinity, after the nearby estate of the Trinity-Sergius Monastery. An icon from the monastery was then placed above the gate. During the Great Northern War at the start of the 18th century, earthworks were built along the former moat, and the guard at the tower was increased, but this proved a short-lived period of martial preparedness. When Napoleon's retreating forces detonated gunpowder mines in the tower as they left, the blast seriously damaged the structure and started a fire that not only ate through joists, but consumed the structure of the clock. The main bell duly fell, smashing through four floors. It took years for the building to be repaired. In 1918, it was taken over by the Red Guards, eventually becoming home to a small detachment of the Kremlin Guard. Today, it contains the Russian Presidential Orchestra's offices and recording studio.

Vasnetsov's evocative picture clearly shows the defensive nature of the Trinity Bridge, anchored at one end by the Kutafiya bastion (here shown with wooden roof, later dispensed with) and the other, the Trinity Tower. (Public domain)

Tsar's (1680s)
The smallest tower, just under 17m tall, the Tsar's Tower was built later than the rest, to replace a wooden watchtower, whose role and bell were then transferred to the Alarm Tower. It was essentially a decorative rather than defensive structure, evoking traditional architectural motifs. It is said that tsars would show themselves to their people from this tower, but that may simply be myth.

Vodovzvodnaya (1488)
In 1633, the 61m-tall Sviblov Tower, named after the Sviblo aristocratic family whose estate adjoined it, was renamed the Water-Lifting Tower, when the Scottish engineer Christopher Galloway fitted it with the first pressure pipe system in Moscow. This pulled water from the Moskva to be distributed through the complex via a network of lead pipes. Originally, though, it was primarily a fortification. It was the second of the brick towers to be built, after Tainitskaya and before Beklemishevskaya, and together the three defined the fortified triangle of the Kremlin. As such, its walls are especially thick – 3m at the base – and a well was dug in the basement in case of a siege. Initially a plain and squat cylindrical tower, the tower went through major changes in the 17th century. First, Galloway built his water wheel, driven by horses walking a circular path inside the tower. Later, the tower acquired a new, four-storey

TODAY'S KREMLIN

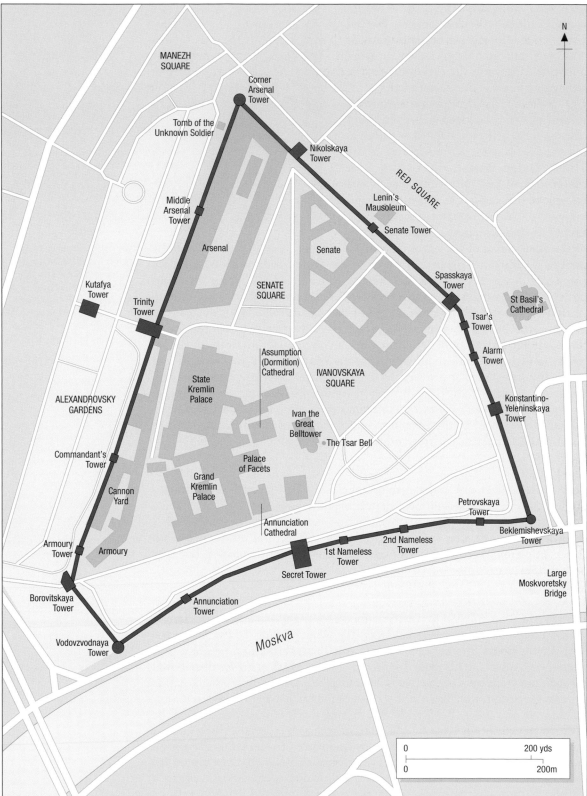

MANEZH SQUARE

N

Corner Arsenal Tower

Tomb of the Unknown Soldier

Nikolskaya Tower

RED SQUARE

Lenin's Mausoleum

Middle Arsenal Tower

Senate Tower

Arsenal

Senate

Spasskaya Tower

Kutafya Tower

SENATE SQUARE

St Basil's Cathedral

Trinity Tower

Tsar's Tower

Assumption (Dormition) Cathedral

Alarm Tower

State Kremlin Palace

IVANOVSKAYA SQUARE

ALEXANDROVSKY GARDENS

Ivan the Great Belltower

Konstantino-Yeleninskaya Tower

The Tsar Bell

Commandant's Tower

Palace of Facets

Cannon Yard

Grand Kremlin Palace

Petrovskaya Tower

Beklemishevskaya Tower

Armoury Tower

Annunciation Cathedral

2nd Nameless Tower

Armoury

1st Nameless Tower

Secret Tower

Large Moskvoretsky Bridge

Borovitskaya Tower

Annunciation Tower

Vodovzvodnaya Tower

Moskva

| 0 | 200 yds |
| 0 | 200m |

58

tower and spire. Successive inspections found the tower's foundations to be in excellent shape, and when, in 1805, the upper stages were repaired, an additional internal wall was built inside them, the space in between being filled with rubble. The idea was to ensure it was fit for modern war, but in 1812 it was blown up from the inside by the French. It was rebuilt, but with more of an eye to elegance, the loopholes being replaced by round and semi-circular windows. Beyond the replacement of a gilded flag weathervane with an illuminated red ruby star in Soviet times, externally it has not changed since.

TODAY'S KREMLIN

At the end of 1991, with the dissolution of the Soviet Union, the Kremlin became the seat of the new Russian Federation. The 1990s saw considerable restoration work (allegedly the vehicle for some industrial-state embezzlement within the Presidential Administration's Property Management Directorate) and, into the 2000s, much of the old tsarist character was restored, including the double-headed eagles on some towers. Churches and monasteries within the walls were also reopened and refurbished. It is again symbolic of state power both at home and around the world and considerable effort is put into maintaining it not just as a working government centre but also a place of beauty and heritage. Indeed, its walls are periodically tinted with red paint to maintain their distinctive hue.

A number of different government and national institutions operate within the Kremlin walls:

• The Presidential Administration (Senate Palace): Although the main offices of the president's powerful personal staff are in Old Square, a short walk away, key staff and those directly responsible for the president's day-to-day routine have offices inside the Kremlin.

• The Grand Kremlin Palace: Now used to host official ceremonies involving the president, and the official residences of both the president and the Patriarch of Moscow and All the Russias.

• The State Kremlin Palace: What was formerly the Palace of Congresses is now used for other major events.

• The Federal Protection Service (FSO): As well as the small Presidential Security Service – a division of the FSO – this agency maintains the Kremlin Guard, also known as the Presidential Regiment.

• Kremlyovsky Catering Agency: This state company not only caters for the staff working in the Kremlin, but also for receptions and major events.

• The Moscow Kremlin State Historical and Cultural Museum-Reserve: The agency responsible for the tourist areas of the complex.

• The Russian Orthodox Church: The Arkhangelsk, Annunciation and Assumption Cathedrals and the Church of the Deposition are all again working religious buildings.

Security is strict, regularly reviewed and constantly upgraded. There is now an extensive network of cameras round the walls and inside the complex, with some of those monitoring people entering the areas open to the public through the Trinity Tower being high-resolution ones connected to advanced facial-recognition systems able to identify suspected terrorists. Mobile phone transmissions within the area are constantly monitored and can be jammed by emitters emplaced around the complex or by shutting down the nearby celltowers, both of which can be done from the security command centre in the Kremlin Commandant's HQ. With drones an increasing concern – flying drones over the centre of Moscow is illegal – the Kremlin is now protected by a GPS spoofing system that makes cellphones and GPS-based navigation systems believe they are elsewhere, typically Vnukovo airport, 30km away. For more serious threats, it reportedly also has a Krasukha-4 ground-based jamming system able to knock drones and even radar-guided missiles out of the sky, and the Kremlin Guard have also tested hand-held anti-drone weapons including the Garpun-M and Pishchal-PRO.

The Presidential Regiment

Security for the Kremlin is the responsibility of the Federal Protection Service. The Presidential Security Service (SBP) is the division of the FSO that provides close protection for the president, and so while its main commitment is wherever 'the Body' (as Kremlin jargon has it) may be, there is a permanent presence also in the Kremlin to maintain security in his offices and quarters.[4] As well as physical security, this extends to the usual panoply of top-tier protection these days, such as constant monitoring of the air in rooms for any signs of potential chemical or biological contaminants and protecting the integrity of their electronics, although cybersecurity is the responsibility of the FSO's SSSI (Special Communications and Information Service). The Special Purpose Garage (GON) has a fleet of over a hundred cars, motorcycles and vans for the president's use, and if that's not fast enough, there's the four-aircraft Presidential Squadron. Both of these are obviously based outside the Kremlin, although there is a helicopter pad in the Tainitsky (Secret) Garden for the Mi-17 helicopter he favours for his occasional 'commutes' from his out-of-town residence at Novo-Ogaryovo.

More generally, Kremlin security is assured by the presence of the Kremlin Guard regiment, which since 1992 has been formally – and rather indigestibly – known as the Independent Red Banner Order of the October Revolution Regiment of the Commandant's Office of the Moscow Kremlin, or simply the Presidential Regiment. It is responsible to the Kremlin Commandant, himself a senior FSO officer, with dual reporting to the director of the FSO and directly to the president.

---

[4]   See ELI 197 *Russian Security and Paramilitary Forces since 1991*

Members of the Presidential Regiment's Cavalry Escort Squadron in Cathedral Square. Note the wave-green summer uniforms. This is the only operational element of the regiment that accepts female recruits. (Sergei Bobylev/TASS via Getty Images)

Although some elements are based and train elsewhere in the city, the regiment's barracks are in the Arsenal building, known as Block 14. Its enclosed courtyard is their parade and exercise ground. The vehicles used by the SBP (the president's motorcade is 12-strong, including an ambulance, vans full of heavily armed officers, a communications van and one or two 7-ton armoured Aurus Senat limousines) are housed near the Borovitsky Gate or in garages under the arches of the Bolshoy Kamenny and Krymsky Bridges. The main stables of the Presidential Cavalry Escort are at Kalininets, a village 55km to the west, while the training bases of the regiment are in the townships of Kupavna and Noginsk to the east of the city.

The regiment has a strength of 5,500 soldiers, all of whom have had to meet demanding physical fitness requirements, must be 175–190cm in height, and have good eyesight and hearing (able to hear a whisper from 6 metres away). They must never have been registered at a psychiatric facility, or a sexually transmitted disease or substance abuse clinic, and must pass a ferocious background check that disqualifies them even if a close relative lives abroad. They wear dark blue uniforms with the FSO's blue-backed service badge, with a dark blue-green parade uniform, or camouflage when not on public-facing duties. For ceremonial duties, the honour guard companies don impressive uniforms based on those of the old Imperial Guard. On parade, they still use SKS carbines, but away from public view and in emergencies, they deploy a full panoply of modern weapons, including 9mm Vityaz-SM SMGs, the 5.45mm AKS-74U assault carbine and AKS-74 and AN-94 rifle, as well as the RPK-74 and PKM machine gun and a series of sniper rifles including the dated SVD, the modern .408 Lobayev OVL03 and the imported British AWM-F rifles chambered for the .338 Lapua Magnum. According to some reports, the regiment may have tested the formidable ShAK-12, a 12.7mm assault weapon designed for FSB special forces, but this was more likely to have been the specialists in the SBP, for whom its terrifying short-range stopping power may be of particular use. The standard sidearm is the high-power 9mm SPS pistol.

Organization of the Presidential Regiment	
Regiment HQ	
Security Company	
Presidential Band	
1st Battalion	2nd Company
	3rd Company
	4th Company
	5th Company
2nd Battalion	6th Company
	7th Company
	8th Company
	9th Company
3rd Battalion	1st Honour Guard Company
	11th Honour Guard Company
	Automotive Company
Presidential Cavalry Escort Battalion	1st Cavalry Squadron
	2nd Cavalry Squadron
	Support Squadron
4th Operational Reserve Battalion	Operational Reserve Company

BIBLIOGRAPHY

Brumfield, William Craft, *A History of Russian Architecture* (Cambridge University Press, 1993)

Devyatov, S. V., *Moskovskii Kreml'* (The Moscow Kremlin) (Kuchkovo Field, 2010)

Devyatov S. V., V. I Zhilyaev and O. K. Kaykova, *Moskovskii Kreml' v gody Velikoi Otechestvennoi voiny* (The Moscow Kremlin during the years of the Great Patriotic War) (Kuchkovo Field, 2010)

Devyatov S. V. and E. V. Zhuravleva, *Moskovskii Kreml' na rubezhe tysyacheletii* (The Moscow Kremlin on the Eve of the Millennium) (PIM, 2010)

Ivanov, Yuri, *Starinnye kreposti Rossii* (Old Fortresses of Russia) (Rusich, 2004)

Karpova Fasce, Ekaterina, 'Gli architetti italiani a Mosca nei secoli XV-XVI', *Quaderni di Scienza della Conservazione* (vol. 4, 2004)

Merridale, Catherine, *Red Fortress* (Metropolitan Books, 2013)

Mikhailov, K., *Unichtozhennyi Kreml'* (The Destroyed Kremlin) (Eksmo, 2007)

Mil'chik, Mikhail and Nikita Andreev, *Kak stroili goroda na Rusi* (How Cities Were Built in Russia) (Kacheli, 2017)

Nossov, Konstantin, *Medieval Russian Fortresses, AD 862–1480* (Osprey, 2007)

Nossov, Konstantin, *Russian Fortresses, 1480–1682* (Osprey, 2006)

Voyce, Arthur, *The Moscow Kremlin: Its history, architecture and art treasures* (University of California Press, 1954)

INDEX

References to images are in **bold**.

1905 Revolution 39–40

ABM (anti-ballistic missile) defences 47
Alarm Tower 45, 48
Alekseyevna, Sophia 34
Aleviz Ditch 18, **19**, 21
Alexander I of Russia, Tsar 36, 37
Alexandrovsky Gardens 4, 35
Algirdas of Lithuania, Prince 15–16
Annunciation Tower 48–49
Armoury 28, 44, 49
Arsenal 18, **19**, **25**, 38, 40–41, 45, **46**

Batu Khan 12
Beklemishevskaya Tower 49–50
Bogolyubsky, Andrei 9, 10
Bolsheviks 40–42
bolverks (outworks) 35, 49, 50, 51
Boris Godunov, Tsar 26, 30
Borovitskaya Tower 6, 50
Borovitsky Gate 60, **61**
Borovitsky Hill 4, 6, 17
Brezhnev, Leonid 50
bunkers 45, 46

cannons 17, **23**, 24, 38
Carezano, Aloisio da 20, 21, 51, 52
Cathedral of the Archangel 22
Cathedral of the Dormition 13, 18, 21
Cathedral Square 6, 18, 22–23, 37, **62**
Catherine II of Russia, Tsarina 54
Chodkiewicz, Hetman Jan Karol 31–32
Christianity 8; *see also* Russian Orthodox Church
Cold War 45–47
Commandant's Tower 51
Committee of State Security (KGB) 46
Copper Coin Riot (1662) 34
Corner Arsenal Tower 24, **25**, 51
Cossacks 31, 32, 37
Crimea 26, 28

Daniil Aleksandrovich, Prince 9, 12
deception (*maskirovka*) 44–45
Devlet-Giray Khan 26, 28, 54
Dmitry I of Moscow, Grand Prince 15, 16–17, 50
Dolgoruky, Yuri 8–9
drones 60
Dubasov, Vice Adm Fyodor 39
Dyakovo culture 6
Dzerzhinsky, Felix 54

Earthern Rampart (*Zemlyannoy Val*) 26

'False Dmitry' 30, 31
Fatyanovo culture 6
Federal Protection Service (FSO) 59
Fioravanti, Ridolfo 'Aristotele' 20, 21
First Nameless Tower 48
Friedrich Wilhelm III of Prussia, Emperor 36
Fyodor I of Russia, Tsar 30
Fyodor III of Russia, Tsar 34

Galloway, Christopher 57
Gilardi, Antonio 54
Glinskaya, Yelena 24
Golden Horde 12, 13, 15, 16–17
Gonsiewski, Col Alexander 31, 32
gorod (fortified settlement) 6, 7, 8, 9–10
Grand Kremlin Palace 38, 59
Great Northern War (1700–21) 35
Great October Revolution (1917) 40–41
Great Patriotic War *see* World War II
guns 17, 28, 46

Heraldic Tower 18, **19**, 36, 51
Herberstein, Sigismund von **25**, 29
Hermogenes, Patriarch 31
Hessel, Gerrits 29
Hitler, Adolf 44

Imperial Guard: Semyonovsky Lifeguard Rgt 40
Independent Red Banner Kremlin KGB Rgt 42, 46
Independent Special Forces Rgt (OPSpN) 42
Italy 18, 20
Ivan I of Moscow, Grand Prince 13
Ivan III (the Great) of Russia, Tsar 18, 20, 21
Ivan IV (the Terrible) of Russia, Tsar 22–23
Ivan the Great Belltower 22, **23**

Kazy-Girey II Khan 26
Kiev 8, 9
Kolomenskoye **12**
Kolomna 12, **21**
Konstantino-Yeleninskaya Tower 52
Kremlin 4–5, 13, 15–17, 35–36
    and 1905 Revolution 39–40
    and Bolsheviks 40–42
    and Cold War 45–47
    and *gorod* 6, **7**, 8, 9–10
    and Ivan the Terrible 22–23
    and Mikhail Romanov 32, **33**
    and modern day **58**, 59–60
    and Napoleon 37–38
    and Poland 30–32
    and red brick 18, **19**, 20–22
    and Soviet Union 42, 44
    and towers 48–54, **55**, 56–57, 58
    and weaponry 28–29
    and World War II 42, **43**, 44–45
Kriviches 8
Kulikovo, battle of (1380) 15, 16
Kutafiya Tower 52–53, 54, **55**
Kutuzov, Marshal Mikhail 36, 37

Latvian Rifles 41, 42
Lenin, Vladimir 40, 45, 54, 56
Lithuania 15–16, 26, 31
Lyalovo culture 6
Lyapunov, Prokopy 31

Maly, Petrok 24
Mantagnana, Lamberti Aloisio da 21–22
maps 29
    modern Kremlin **58**
    Moscow's walls **27**
    rise of the Muscovite state **14**
Matveyev, Artamon 34
Metro-2 transport system 46–47
Middle Arsenal Tower **46**, 53
Mikhail Romanov of Russia, Tsar 32, **33**
militias 10, 31–32
Miloslavskies 34
Min, Gen Georgy 40
Minin, Kuzma 31, **32**
Mongols 5, 10, **11**, 12–13
Mortier, Marshal Édouard 37
Moscow 8–9, 24–26, **27**, 36–38
    map **14**
    see also Kremlin
Moscow Kremlin State Historical and Cultural Museum-Reserve 59
Moscow Military Revolutionary Committee (MVRK) 40, 41
Moskva River 4, 6
Moss Tower (Sumy) **9**
Murat, Marshal Prince Joachim-Napoléon 37

Napoleon 5, 36–38, 53
Naryshkins 34
Nazi Germany 5, 44
Neglinnaya River 4, 6, 21, 35
Nemtsov, Boris **50**
Nevsky, Alexander 12
Nicholas I of Russia, Tsar 38
Nikolskaya Tower 53
Novgorod 8

Oleg 9
Oruj Bek Bayat 29
Ottoman Empire 26

Paleologue, Sofia 18
People's Commissariat for Internal Affairs (NKVD) 42
Peter the Great of Russia, Tsar 29, 34–35, 49, 54, 56
Petrovskaya Tower 18, **19**, 53–54
Poland 26, 30–32
Popov, Gavriil 46
posad (mercantile quarter) 24
Pozharsky, Prince Dmitry 31, 32
Presidential Administration 59
Presidential Regiment 5, **41**, 60, 62–63
Putin, Vladimir 4, **38**, 47
Pyotr, Metropolitan 13, 18

Red Army **40**, 41
Red Porch 21, **22**
Red Square 4, **42**, 45
Romanov dynasty 4, 30
Romodanovsky, Prince General Grigory 34
Rostopchin, Count Fyodor 37
Ruffo, Marco 20, 21
Rurik 9
Russian Orthodox Church 13, 18, 31, 42, 59
Russo-Japanese War (1904–5) 39

St Petersburg 4, 29, 34–35, 37, 38
    and 'Bloody Sunday' massacre 39
    and Bolsheviks 40
Second Nameless Tower 48
Secret Tower 18, **19**, 54
security 59–60, **61**
Segur, Count Philip de 36, 37
Senate Tower 54
Seven-Headed Tower (Semiverkhaya) 25–26
Sigismund III of Poland, King 30
Sokolov, Fyodor 38
Solari, Pietro 20, 56
Spasskaya Tower 41, 42, **43**, 45, 56
Spassky Gate 18, **19**
Stalin, Joseph 45, 46, 54
State Kremlin Palace 59
Streltsy ('Shooters') (standing army) 18, **19**, 23, 24, 28–29, 32, 34
    and executions 35
    and Konstantino-Yeleninskaya Tower 52
Strus, Mikolai 32
Svyatoslav Olgovich, Prince 8–9
Sweden 26, 35

Tainitskaya Tower **54**
Tatars 26, 28
Tokhtamysh Khan 16–17
Tolbuzin, Semyon 20
Tomb of the Unknown Soldier **20**
towers 13, 21, 48–54, **55**, 56–57, 58
Trinity Tower 54, **55**, 56–57
Tsar Bell **35**
Tsar's Tower 57
Tudan 10, **11**, 12, 13
tunnels 45

Varangians (Vikings) 9
Vasily III, Grand Duke 50
Vasily IV Shuisky, Tsar 30–31
Victory Day **4**, **52**, 56
Viskovsky, Col Nikolai 40
Vladimir of Kiev, Prince 8
Vodovzvodnaya Tower 18, **19**, 57, 59
Vyatiches 6, 8

walls 20–21, 24–25
White City (*Bely Gorod*) 25–26
Wladyslaw IV, Crown Prince 31
Wooden City (*Skorodom*) 26
World War II (1939–45) 42, **43**, 44–45